A SAMPLE OF A FATHER'S MOST MEMORABLE WORDS

"I suppose it won't be long until I lose you to some funny looking gink who you think is wonderful because he is so romantic looking in the evening and wears his mother's pearl earrings for dress-shirt buttons, because he loves her so. . . . However, perhaps you'll use your head and wait until you are at least twenty-one."
—*Jacqueline Bouvier Kennedy Onassis*'s father, Jack Vernon Bouvier, III

"The way it is in our family, we try to make something happen rather than waiting for it to happen. We believe the surest way is to work toward making it happen."   —*Michael Jordan*'s father, James Jordan

"Mind you, don't go looking for fights, but if you find yourself in one, make damn sure you win."   —*John Wayne*'s father, Clyde Morrison

"All right, I'll give you fifty dollars to help pay your expenses for a couple of weeks, until you recover from this madness, but that's the last penny you'll get from me until you do something respectable."
—*Katharine Hepburn*'s father, Dr. Norval Thomas Hepburn

DAVID HORNFISCHER is the Vice President for Administration and Finance at Berklee College of Music in Boston, and ELSA HORNFISCHER is a registered nurse. They live in Framingham, Massachusetts, and have two married children and one grandson. They have had fathers for over 50 years, and David has been one for 30 years. This is their second book.

Father Knew Best

Wit and Wisdom from the Dads of Celebrities

David and Elsa Hornfischer

A PLUME BOOK

PLUME
Published by the Penguin Group
Penguin Books USA Inc., 375 Hudson Street, New York, New York 10014, U.S.A.
Penguin Books Ltd, 27 Wrights Lane, London W8 5TZ, England
Penguin Books Australia Ltd, Ringwood, Victoria, Australia
Penguin Books Canada Ltd, 10 Alcorn Avenue, Toronto, Ontario, Canada M4V 3B2
Penguin Books (N.Z.) Ltd, 182–190 Wairau Road, Auckland 10, New Zealand

Penguin Books Ltd, Registered Offices:
Harmondsworth, Middlesex, England

First published by Plume, an imprint of Dutton Signet,
a division of Penguin Books USA Inc.

First Printing, May, 1997
1 3 5 7 9 10 8 6 4 2

 REGISTERED TRADEMARK—MARCA REGISTRADA

LIBRARY OF CONGRESS CATALOGING-IN-PUBLICATION DATA
Hornfischer, David.
Father knew best : wit and wisdom from the dads of celebrities /
David & Elsa Hornfischer.
p.   cm.
ISBN 0-452-27772-8 (alk. paper)
1. Fathers—Quotations, maxims, etc.   2. Fathers—United States—
Anecdotes.   I. Hornfischer, Elsa.   II. Title.
PN6084.F3H67   1997
306.874'2—dc21   96-49691
CIP

Printed in the United States of America
Set in New Caledonia
Designed by Jesse Cohen

BOOKS ARE AVAILABLE AT QUANTITY DISCOUNTS WHEN USED TO PROMOTE PRODUCTS OR SERVICES. FOR IN-FORMATION PLEASE WRITE TO PREMIUM MARKETING DIVISION, PENGUIN BOOKS USA INC., 375 HUDSON STREET, NEW YORK, NEW YORK 10014.

this book is dedicated

To the fathers
who brought life
to these pages

They did the best they could
with what they had
and it made a difference

To our fathers
Raymond and Ernest
for over sixty years
of devotion

To the men close to us
Jim, Marcel, Jacob
and Paul

They make a difference

ACKNOWLEDGMENTS

Writing an acknowledgment for a second book is a bit like sending announcements following the birth of your second child: The special people you recognize are just as special the second time around. In this case, our literary agent son, Jim Hornfischer, who reminds us that he does not get paid to "coddle my clients," deserves the lion's share of our thanks for his sharp and helpful advice. Our editor, Danielle Perez, among the publishing experts at Penguin/Plume, deserves a big thank-you for helping us translate the successful theme of *Mother Knew Best* to *Father Knew Best*. Thank you also to Penguin publicist Yvonne Orteig and her assistant, Victoria Hardy.

Beyond the publishing world, a special thanks goes out to our family. Our daughter, Amy, reminds Dave periodically of the fatherly messages, both good and bad, that he has imparted to her over the years, while her husband, Marcel, is seeing firsthand the challenge of fathering our grandson, Jacob. And here's a special thank-you to Jim's wife, Sharon, who is a precious addition to our family.

Acknowledgment of a book about fathers, however, must give primary thanks to our own. Dave certainly got his sense of ambition and responsibility from his hardworking father, Raymond John Hornfischer, who left high school during the Depression in order to support his parents. He reminded Dave regularly of the benefits of a college education, and sacrificed to make it possible. Elsa's father, Ernest Boettcher Bozenhard, gave her the perspective to think more globally in their very ordinary neighborhood while passing along his lifetime love of the written word.

Finally, a special thank-you to the employees and supporters of the Framingham Public Library. They must have wondered why we were taking out so many biographies! During the course of researching both books, we came to understand in an entirely new way the value and importance of a well-run and well-stocked public library.

INTRODUCTION

Norman Schwarzkopf described him as a "true patriot." Michael Jordan said he was "my best friend." He was Edith Wharton's "soul mate" and Rush Limbaugh's "hero." Donald Trump described him as his "most important influence." He was Paul McCartney's "strongest musical influence." F. Scott Fitzgerald may have said it most simply—"I love my father."

Fathers are a unique lens through which to view their children, and all the more when their children are well-known to us all. But though our culture is obsessed with celebrities, we seldom learn anything about their deepest personal lives. In his 1985 book, *America*, Andy Warhol addresses our fascination with the famous. "No matter how perfectly someone's got their public personality going, it's never as good as their real life." What better way to find out more about celebrities' real lives than through their fathers?

In the following pages, we have assembled 101 real-life stories of celebrities and their fathers. As we did our research, we delighted in the variety, poignance, and timelessness of these tales. We also found that, much as in our first book, *Mother Knew Best*, the stories tended to classify themselves according to seven virtues passed along from parent to child: Ambition, Courage, Devotion, Faith, Perspective, Responsibility, and Self-discipline. As we found with the celebrities featured in *Mother Knew Best*, the childhood lessons in virtue proved to be early foundations for the celebrities' later success.

As the book evolved, we had occasion to reflect also on the larger issue of fatherhood. What surprised us most as we gathered the stories across the centuries was that the fatherly messages were more alike than different. From the examples of Emily Dickinson and Thomas Jefferson to those of Sally Ride and Jerry Seinfeld, these childhood lessons not only fell into our seven categories, but resounded with a father's hope for his child's future success.

During depressions and wars, during times of political turmoil, or as a result of divorce or death, many fathers were absent or distracted. Oprah Winfrey spent very little time with her father until she was fourteen. He then entered her life, loved her enough to enforce some rules, and changed her life forever. George Burns' immigrant father worked twelve-hour days in a sweatshop while supporting his family the best he could. Some fathers passed away when their children were very young. Eleanor Roosevelt's father died when she was ten, but he remained her lifelong inspiration. Dr. Ruth Westheimer's father perished in a concentration camp, leaving letters of love that his daughter still treasures. Fathers who either worked at home, on a farm, in a family business, or had regular work hours were generally more available to their children. Sid Caesar worked alongside his father in their luncheonette in Yonkers. John M. Studebaker labored with his father and brothers as a blacksmith and wagon maker, while Ben Franklin apprenticed as a candle maker in his father's workshop in Boston.

In some of the stories, the father was busy "doing," either working hard at his job, at war, or involved in his own activities, serving primarily as a model of behavior for his child. In other stories, the father spent more of his time supporting, disciplining, or guiding the child. But whether modeling behaviors or more directly supporting or disciplining their children, our fathers of celebrities all resembled one another in two ways: They communicated a meaningful message to their children, and they were committed to their roles as fathers.

While many profess to know "the way" to be a good father, Bill Cosby in his book *Fatherhood* refuses to give "absolute rules because there are none." We profess, after researching this book, that there are many ways to "father" as long as commitment is the common denominator and a meaningful message results. In *Fatherhood in America*, Robert L. Griswold describes a benefit of successful fatherhood: "How men think about fatherhood helps us understand how they think about themselves as men."

From Picasso, who always said that he thought of his father every time he drew a male figure, to Emily Dickinson, who wrote a sorrowful lament at her father's death, "Home is so far from Home, since my Father died," these stories will strike a universal chord in anyone fortunate enough to have had a loving father in their lives. May you cherish yours, while recognizing the power and influence of fatherhood "done well."

—David and Elsa Hornfischer
August 1996

Father
Knew
Best

AMBITION

Sid Caeser
Barbara Mandrell
Wolfgang Amadeus Mozart
Michael Jordan
Clint Eastwood
John Adams
Julie Andrews
Carl Yastrzemski
Roy Rogers
Conrad Hilton
Donald Trump
Dean Martin
F. Scott Fitzgerald
Monica Seles
Charles Dickens
Emily Post
Miles Davis
A. J. Foyt Jr.
Mary Cassatt

AMBITION

*F*athers, especially fathers who pride themselves on being ambitious, usually want to see the same ambition reflected in their children. They want their children to work hard in school, to get good grades, to find a career focus, and to pursue it diligently. In real life, however, it is rarely that simple. In the quest for attainment or direction, children often stumble, and when they do, they often find out more about life. Fathers who continue to nudge, inspire, or encourage their children in between falls eventually get their message across.

Some fathers pursue their own goal, carrying along a fascinated and hardworking child. In effect, the father achieves in an area that the child comes to value. Toddler Wolfgang Amadeus Mozart watched as his musician father taught his sister to play the piano. By the age of four, young Mozart had written his first concerto, to his father's delight, and spent the early years of his career supported and guided by his father. After the New York City currency panic of 1907, Conrad Hilton and his father worked long and hard at starting a hotel in their adobe home in New Mexico, launching a legacy that continues today.

Sometimes, a child's path to achievement wanders a little along the way, but the father eventually lives to see his child's success. Young Michael Jordan was on academic suspension as a student in high school. His father, the son of a hardworking share-cropper, just couldn't understand his son's lack of ambition. Once, however, he reminded Michael that college was out of the picture unless his grades improved, Michael "woke up" and studied hard. The rest is sports history.

Some fathers quietly pass along a message of ambition, only to see it flower later in their children's life. Emily Post never forgot the message that her architect father shared with her. He equated living a life to building a life, explaining, "If you know the laws and respect them, you can't help building well." Years later, Emily Post's seven-hundred-page book on the rules of eti-quette would top the best-seller list.

Some fathers nudge and push their children in ways the chil-dren don't appreciate until they become adults. Julie Andrews' musical stepfather loved music and recognized her talent early. He nudged his somewhat reluctant stepdaughter to take lessons and perform with his vaudeville act. Much later, as an adult, a grateful Julie Andrews credited her stepfather with giving her an identity that she would have been "mixed up" without.

Stories of ambition take many shapes and many forms—the message is passed along from father to child in different ways. Each child in this book understood and processed this verbal or nonverbal message, turning it into the drive necessary to become a celebrity adult.

*F*or the proud man from Poland struggling to make a living in Yonkers, this had to matter. After all, he had a twenty-four-hour luncheonette to run in this factory town; knew most everybody; and played poker and pinochle with the other businessmen, the Collinses and Dumans being the most successful of the bunch. It wasn't easy to grow up in this immigrant neighborhood and make a name for yourself.

Max Caesar, sporting an Anglican name that was assigned to him at Ellis Island, worked hard and long and was proud of it. He'd often get up at 2 A.M., go to the produce market, and by 4 A.M. be back in time to serve breakfast at the luncheonette. In the years after World War I, financial survival was the name of the game. The business finally went bankrupt in 1935, when Sid was thirteen, but Max courageously picked himself up, dusted himself off, and started all over again. By the time he was old and tired, he had survived three luncheonettes and a novelty store. Sid always referred to him as a symbol of strength.

Sid was always curious about the luncheonette, which he recalled "gobbled up" his family for tremendous lengths of time, and as he grew older he'd drop in at lunch, where he would thrill at hearing accents from all over the world. Soon he began imitating the accents with remarkable clarity, to the delight of the patrons—except when they concentrated on what he was *saying* (the rhythm and cadence were just perfect) and realized that they couldn't understand a word of it!

Sid took up the saxophone, which he'd mastered well enough by his teenage years to contribute to the family coffers. Once he discovered comedy, however, his life changed. In a discipline that at the time depended on slapstick and visual gags, Sid instead developed routines centered on everyday life and the people he had seen in his father's luncheonette.

It didn't take long for comedian Sid Caesar to make a name for himself. At the height of his career, he starred in *Your Show of Shows* and *Caesar's Hour* on television, performing with Imogene Coca, Carl Reiner, and others. By 1978, however, the occasional drinking that had started in the forties had escalated to constant drinking, with the addition now of pills. His career and his life were at risk. While performing in Regina, Saskatchewan, he collapsed and was admitted to the hospital there. He had hit bottom.

With a courage and determination inspired by his father, Sid started his path to recovery from substance abuse. He joined a health club in Beverly Hills and wrote his story, dedicated to his wife and children. In his autobiography, Sid gave his family a forum to share their difficulties with his addiction. Sid hoped that these personal testimonies would give courage to others and that they might learn to banish their demons as he did.

SOURCE:
Where Have I Been? An Autobiography, Sid Caesar with Bill Davidson (Crown Publishers, New York, 1982).

FAMOUS CHILD: Barbara Mandrell

FATHER'S NAME: Irby Mandrell

PAPA ASKED: *"Is she learning enough arithmetic to be able to count money and figure the percentages?"*

Barbara's math teacher answered in the affirmative.

"Well, that's great, because all I ever expect her to do is play music, count money, and figure percentages."

*I*rby Mandrell had left school as a teenager in order to support his family, later joining the Navy medical corps in World War II and after that working long days in the oil fields. Eventually, he became a policeman, then left law enforcement and started his own music store. Once he had organized the Mandrell Family Band, however, Irby knew where his family was going. And for his daughter Barbara, counting money and figuring percentages was all the math she needed to know.

Always close to her father, Barbara remembers that she loved seeing the police car in front of their house in Corpus Christi, Texas, for it meant that her father was there. And when he was there, the house filled with the sound of music. By eleven, Barbara had performed in Las Vegas with her steel guitar and saxophone, instruments usually played by men. For Barbara, playing these instruments symbolized the feminist message passed along by her father, who had told her, "Once you've qualified yourself, don't let anybody say you can't do it because you're a girl."

And "do it" she did. In a family band dominated by the talents of Barbara and her sisters, Louise and Irlene, Barbara Mandrell landed a television variety show before a serious head-on car accident changed her life. But with the strong constitution of her dad and generations of resilient Mandrells, Barbara recovered and courageously continued her career.

Barbara describes her father's look as the "Mandrell Look" —which some, she says, call "arrogance but I call confidence." She adds, "I'm supposed to be a big girl now, but when there's a problem, I feel better just knowing I can call on the man with the Mandrell Look."

SOURCE:
Get to the Heart—My Story, Barbara Mandrell with George Vecsey (Bantam Books, New York, 1990).

FAMOUS CHILD: Wolfgang Amadeus Mozart

FATHER'S NAME: Leopold Mozart

PAPA SAID: *"Nannerl is finished for the day, and you too! Off with you!"*

*W*hen Wolfgang's sister, Nannerl, was seven years old, Leopold began teaching her the piano while three-year-old Wolfgang looked on, fascinated with the sounds as he played with his blocks. At times, he stopped playing to concentrate and then, after she'd left the piano, would reproduce the sounds he had heard. When unsuccessful, he would cry in disappointment, and by the next day he'd have figured out how to remedy his mistake. Leopold's curt remark, made to his eager three-year-old son as he interrupted Nannerl's music lesson, helped fuel the beginnings of a seed of burning ambition in his son, as did the piano lessons that Leopold, half in fun, provided for Wolfgang beginning at the age of four.

Born in 1756 in Salzburg, Austria, Mozart was one of two children. The Mozart home was a happy one, filled with pets, plants in the windows, and frequent visitors, who often brought their instruments and filled the home with sound. Leopold, assistant conductor to the orchestra in Salzburg, wore formal dress on most occasions, having attained a social level well above that of his more modest relatives.

One day, Leopold came home accompanied by court trumpeter Andreas Schachtner and found young Mozart upstairs, knee-deep in music paper, ink, and pen, putting the finishing touches on a "concerto." Leopold studied the four-year-old's score, only to hand the document to Schachtner, tearfully observing, "The child has not only written a concerto, but one so difficult that nobody can possibly play it." "*Aber ja*, Papa, you are right!" Wolfgang responded. "It is so hard—that is why it is a concerto. You must practice it until it is perfect."

With a strong musical ambition in his soul, young Mozart "played" with his talent, reaching higher and higher levels of accomplishment. By the age of six, Mozart and his family went on the road and played all over Europe, attracting attention wherever they went.

From original minuets composed beginning at the age of five

to symphonies composed starting at nine, Mozart went on to write his first opera at twelve and to become court organist in Salzburg at twenty-three. By the time of his premature death in 1791, there were an ambitious 626 cataloged works attributed to him.

SOURCE:
Mozart, Marcia Davenport (Charles Scribner's Sons, New York, 1932).

FAMOUS CHILD: Michael Jordan

FATHER'S NAME: James Jordan

PAPA SAID: *"The way it is in our family, we try to make something happen rather than waiting for it to happen. We believe the surest way is to work toward making it happen."*

*F*or James Jordan, son of a poor Carolina sharecropper, hard work was important. James worked in the tobacco fields as a child and later as a forklift operator with General Electric, where he worked his way up to the position of supervisor. However, no matter how hard he tried, he had trouble transferring his work ethic to his son, Michael. James recalled how Michael would often even turn over his allowance to his brothers, sisters, or friends if they would do his chores.

The turnaround came when Michael, as a high school sophomore, was cut from the varsity basketball team. Shocked, Michael rededicated himself to a stringent practice regimen. He would practice basketball four hours a day—and all day on weekends. Of course, such single-minded determination proved to be a detriment to his schoolwork. Just as his game was coming around, Michael found himself on academic suspension. But he wasn't quick to catch the implications of his failure. When his father asked him about his goals, Michael mentioned playing big-time college basketball. "How can you make it to college," asked James, "if you are not going to graduate from high school?"

With a determination and ambition modeled by his dad, Michael Jordan woke up. He began working hard in school. By summer, he was accepted to a summer basketball camp, where his performance drew attention from many college coaches. He enrolled at the University of North Carolina and was soon a key member of the 1982 Tar Heel national championship team, and an all-American.

With the approval of his father, Michael left college after his junior year to play professional basketball. Michael Jordan's play helped the Chicago Bulls win three consecutive championships from 1990 to 1992, while Jordan personally won seven NBA scoring championships, three Most Valuable Player awards, and a second Olympic gold medal as a member of the 1992 Dream Team. His father, whom Michael called his "best friend," was a constant companion throughout his school and professional career.

In 1993, millions of Americans were shocked and saddened when James was found murdered at an interstate rest stop, the apparent victim of a botched robbery attempt. And another shock was in store, when Michael claimed that he had nothing more to accomplish in basketball and announced his retirement from the NBA to become a minor-league baseball player. While many have speculated his reasons for this action, underlying it was probably his father's advice: "You never know what you can accomplish until you try," and "It's never too late to do anything you want to."

Michael has since returned to basketball, perhaps motivated by another message from his dad, an observation few dispute: "I've got to believe one thing. One day God was sitting around and decided to make Himself the perfect basketball player. He gave him a little hardship early in life to make him appreciate what he would earn in the end, and called him Michael Jordan."

SOURCES:
Michael Jordan, Sean Dolan (Chelsea House Publishers, New York, 1994).
Michael Jordan: Star Guard, Ron Knapp (Enslow Publishers, Hillside, New Jersey, 1994).
Michael Jordan, Robert Lipsyte (Harper Trophy, New York, 1994).

FAMOUS CHILD: Clint Eastwood

FATHER'S NAME: Clinton Eastwood Sr.

PAPA SAID: *"Nothing comes from nothing and don't plan on anything, because no one gives you anything in life."*

*T*he actor-director known for the classic line "Go ahead, make my day" in the 1983 movie *Sudden Impact* learned at an early age that he would need to muster enough ambition to make his own way in life. Born in San Francisco in 1930, Clint grew up during the Depression as his father, a stock and bond salesman, struggled to keep the family together. Clint, who later made over 250 episodes of the 1960s TV western series *Rawhide*, learned early the importance of a work ethic as he watched his father move from job to job and the family move from town to town in the American West.

Eastwood explained to biographer Douglas Thompson,

"When I look back I know Dad had to think pretty fast at times because there were a lot of people out of work in America around the time I was born." While Depression-era life may have inspired Eastwood's work ethic (he once made three movies in a thirty-month period), Thompson indicates that moving frequently probably also contributed to what he calls the "lone wolf" personality that is a characteristic of many of his movie roles.

Eastwood admitted, "I'm inclined toward the underdog. I guess I've always been rebellious in that way. I think it had to do with how I was raised." To illustrate the point, the man who was Dirty Harry recalled a quote from his dad: "Show 'em what you can do and don't worry about what you are gonna get. Say you'll work for free and make yourself invaluable."

In addition to his acting and directing, in 1986 Eastwood was elected to the $200-per-month position of mayor of Carmel, California, on a platform of less government intervention. Recalling his father's advice, Eastwood states, "People expect more from Big Daddy government, more from Big Daddy charity. In my young days that kind of society never existed. That philosophy never got you anywhere."

SOURCE:
Clint Eastwood—Riding High, Douglas Thompson (Contemporary Books, Chicago, 1992).

FAMOUS CHILD: John Adams

FATHER'S NAME: John Adams Sr.

PAPA SAID: *"What would you do, child? Be a farmer? I will shew you what it is to be a farmer!"*

John Adams Sr. had a problem: His firstborn wasn't doing well in school. Young John disliked his schoolmaster, "the most indolent Man I ever knew." In his own eighteenth-century-style words, John described his "disgust to Schools, to books and to study and I spent my time as idle Children do in making and sailing boats and Ships upon the Ponds and Brooks, in making and flying Kites, in driving hoops, playing marbles, playing Quoits, Wrestling, Swimming, Skaiting and above all in shooting, to which Diversion I was addicted to a degree of Ardor which I know not that I ever felt for any other Business, Study, or Amusement." No, studying did not make John's list.

John Adams Sr. was upset and was afraid that young John would end up a farmer. In an effort to prove how difficult this calling could be, John Senior had his son accompany him "on the Penny ferry to help him get thatch," a task which took the better part of a day. That evening John Senior asked his son how he had liked it, prompting young John's reply that although it was "very hard and very muddy," he liked it very well. John Senior quickly responded, "Ay, but I don't like it so well: So you shall go to school today."

Encouraged and nudged by his father, John Adams taught himself at home from a copy of *Cocker's Decimal Arithmetick*, readily passed his peers at public school, and prepared to enter Harvard. He anxiously set off on his horse alone, tempted to turn back toward home, but "foreseeing the Grief of my father and apprehending he would . . . be offended with me, I aroused myself, and collected the Resolution enough to proceed."

In his years at Harvard, John Adams developed a keen interest in public affairs and law. Upon graduating, he taught school while studying law, then built a legal practice, later serving as counsel to the town of Boston in the "Stamp Act crisis." With his cousin Samuel Adams, John supported the cause of liberty by protesting royal authority in the colonies, which led to the birth of the revolutionary group Sons of Liberty.

As a young father, John Adams wrote to his wife, Abigail, on parenting: "Let us teach them not only to do virtuously, but to excel. To excel they must be taught to be steady, active, and industrious."

During the American Revolution, John Adams resigned his law practice and served as a Massachusetts delegate to the First Continental Congress in Philadelphia, where he helped draft the Declaration of Independence, earning from Thomas Jefferson the title of Colossus of Independence. John Adams served as second President of the United States before dying at ninety years of age on July 4, 1826, the same day as Thomas Jefferson, on the fiftieth anniversary of the Declaration of Independence.

SOURCE:
John Adams—A Biography in His Own Words, edited by James Bishop Peabody (published by Newsweek Book Division, New York, and distributed by Harper & Row, New York, 1973).

FAMOUS CHILD:	Julie Andrews (Julia Elizabeth Wells)
FATHER'S NAME:	Edward "Ted" Wells
STEPFATHER'S NAME:	Ted "Pop" Andrews

PAPA SAID: *"With the war work taking up so much of my time, I could not do my duty to both of them as a father."*

"STEPFATHER—'POP'—thundered across my childhood. My mum wanted me to call him Uncle Ted, which I was opposed to instantly," Julie Andrews recalls. Her birth father and her mother had divorced when she was little. Realizing early that Julie belonged on stage, Edward said that "being in the theater themselves, they [Julie's mom and stepfather] were better equipped than I to pay for her training," and he voluntarily relinquished custody of six-year-old Julie to them.

Ted "Pop" Andrews and Julie's mother performed a vaudeville act—the Canadian Troubadour, Songs and a Guitar—with Ted singing in his rich tenor voice and Julie's mother playing the piano. Then Pop, described by Julie as "colorful and noisy as show business itself," sent her at the age of seven to singing lessons. He had discovered her voice as he led a cappella singing in a World War II bomb shelter in England. Pop was excited and "forced her to develop her talent," according to author Robert Windeler. Although Julie as a child always resented her stepfather's "pushing nature," she would one day describe herself as "grateful that he had made me take singing lessons. It gave me an identity which later became very necessary." People have always associated Julie's singing talent with the vocal talent of Ted Andrews, but, in truth, Julie says, "there were no vocal musicians in my family."

At ten, Julie stood on a beer crate to reach the microphone to sing her first solo and also sang duets with her mother and stepfather in their act. It was Pop who exposed Julie to her first musical, *South Pacific*, which made a deep impression on her. By twelve, after Pop decided she was ready for a serious career, Julie obtained a "year's run" at a club, and thought she was the "luckiest girl alive." By the age of thirteen, Julie Andrews was selected to perform before royalty, the youngest singer ever so honored, and by nineteen she was a Broadway star. According to Windeler, Julie and her stepfather, Pop, "shared a profession—one that in a real sense he had given her."

SOURCE:
Julie Andrews—A Biography, Robert Windeler (G. P. Putnam's Sons, New York, 1970).

FAMOUS CHILD:	Carl Yastrzemski
FATHER'S NAME:	Carl Yastrzemski Sr.
PAPA SAID:	*"Sign with the Red Sox or go back to school."*

With those ten words in 1958, Carl Senior set in place a baseball career that spanned twenty-three major-league seasons with the Boston Red Sox and eventually led to his son's induction into the Baseball Hall of Fame.

Baseball was a major part of the Yastrzemski family culture. Carl Junior recalls, "After the long hours we all put in on the farm, athletics were our relaxation, and we worked hard to relax." That "work" was largely centered on the family baseball team, the Bridgehampton [New York] White Eagles, which Carl's dad had organized and which consisted of the Yastrzemskis and their cousins, the Skoniecznys. Carl started out as the batboy, but by the time he was fifteen he was a player, competing three times a week against much older players. He speculates that his dad probably kept the White Eagles going into his forties so he could play alongside his son.

Yaz, as Carl was later known, states in his autobiography, "Dad was never a stage father. We'd discuss batting, but the only thing he'd ever correct me on was swinging at bad pitches." He goes on to say, "He didn't correct me, but he certainly practiced with me. Sports were as much a part of my life as school or working on the farm."

Carl attracted major-league scouts, who soon found out that the road to Carl went through his dad, who knew what he wanted. After his father turned down a $60,000 offer from the Yankees, who would not raise their offer to $100,000, Carl enrolled at Notre Dame. While he could not play baseball as a freshman, his name was still on the lists of major-league scouts, who continued to up their offers. When the Red Sox offered $108,000 and said they would pay for his college education, his father agreed to sign. Carl Senior notes that he probably accepted less money from the Boston Red Sox than he could have gotten from other teams so that he'd get the chance to see his son play, Boston being within driving distance of Long Island. By the end of Yaz's Red Sox career, he had played in a record 3,308 games.

Yaz, Little League baseball, and the Baseball Hall of Fame were all born in 1939. In 1989, as all three celebrated their fiftieth birthdays, Carl became the first former Little League player to be inducted into the Hall of Fame. In his acceptance speech Yaz introduced his dad, stating, "Take my father. Super athlete himself. Possessing all the talent and dedication needed to make the big leagues but living at the time of the Depression. He had to suppress his own desires in order that his family could survive and prosper, so he worked and labored toward that end. If ever there's living proof that some people make sacrifices for others, it's my dad."

SOURCES:

Yaz, Baseball, the Wall and Me, Carl Yastrzemski and Gerald Eskenazi (Doubleday, New York, 1990).

Speech text from Yaz World Wide Web page at http://www.epix.net/~brett/yazhof.html

Page maintained by Brett Freedman, brett@epix.net. Created: 9/12/95

FAMOUS CHILD:	Roy Rogers (Leonard Slye)
FATHER'S NAME:	Andy Slye
PAPA SAID:	*"Son, let's quit our jobs and go to California."*

For the first eight years of Leonard Slye's life, he lived in a houseboat made by his father and blind Uncle Bill. The close-knit but poor family then moved to Duck Run, Ohio, where Roy Rogers related later, the family "lived the book *Grapes of Wrath*." Because his father worked in a shoe factory during the week and only came home for a weekend every two weeks, Leonard was responsible at a young age for the farm. The family's evening music sessions with guitar and mandolin were the only entertainment to be had. Leonard not only played the guitar, but called square dances at the age of ten. At sixteen, he went to work at the shoe factory where his father worked, but the Depression presented little opportunity for the family, prompting Andy Slye's suggestion that they move to California. Luckily, Leonard had saved ninety dollars, which would cover the cost of gas.

In California, the family's fortunes improved after eighteen-year-old Leonard's performance on an amateur radio show. Only days later, he was called and offered a job singing and playing with the group Rocky Mountaineers and subsequently performed throughout the Southwest. It wasn't long before Leonard Slye, renamed Roy Rogers, was discovered by Hollywood, and by the end of his career, the singing cowboy had made eighty-one westerns for Republic Pictures and a hundred films for television.

He and his costar wife, Dale Evans, parented nine children, including four by adoption and one foster child. Roy relates, "The best part of my life is my family."

SOURCE:
Roy Rogers—King of the Cowboys, Georgia Morris and Mark Pollard (Collins Publishers, San Francisco, 1994).

FAMOUS CHILD: Conrad Hilton

FATHER'S NAME: Augustus Holver Hilton (Gus)

PAPA SAID: *"All right. I guess you'll be worth twenty-five dollars a month on a full-time basis."*

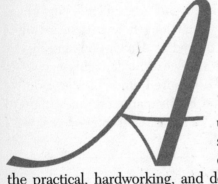

ugustus Hilton listened as his son, Conrad, explained that he didn't want to go to school. For the practical, hardworking, and down-to-earth Augustus, formal education wasn't important. Conrad Hilton explained later that his father responded "much as if I had announced that I did not intend to go to a parade." After all, if Conrad stayed home and worked in the family business, Augustus' own burden would be easier to bear.

To Norwegian immigrant Augustus Hilton, the wild west held not only adventure but also unlimited opportunity for work—especially if you played at it. Described by Conrad as a man with vision "whose work and play were one and the same thing," Augustus spent fourteen-hour days in his trading post and general store along the Rio Grande River in the territory of New Mexico, supplying Spaniards, Mexicans, Indians, trappers, and miners as they passed by. The close, hardworking family of ten lived and worked out of the one-story, rambling adobe building.

After the New York City currency panic of 1907, the Hilton family faced a severe financial crisis, with a significant amount of money owed to creditors and suppliers. The family got together and defined four significant strengths: There was stock on the store shelves; each family member was a hard worker; they owned the large, rambling, adobe store in which they also lived; and the mother of the household was a good cook. With these four strengths as a base, the ambitious family quickly got out of debt, and succeeded in "birthing" a hotel chain in the process that outlived every original member of the family.

Following Gus' death in an auto accident in 1919, Conrad Hilton related, "After thirty-six years of high adventure in the West, sixty-four years of active living, Gus had died on his way to work. He would have had it that way."

SOURCE:
Be My Guest, Conrad Hilton (Prentice Hall Press, New York, 1957).

FAMOUS CHILD:	Donald Trump
FATHER'S NAME:	Fred Trump

PAPA SAID: *"The most important thing in life is to love what you're doing, because that's the only way you'll ever be really good at it."*

Calling his dad his "most important influence," Donald Trump took his advice to heart, describing how much he loves making a deal. "I do it to do it. Deals are my art form."

Donald's father, Fred Trump, became the "man of the house" at the age of eleven, when his own father died. Focused and ambitious, he initially took odd jobs and later registered for evening classes in carpentry. At the age of sixteen, he built a two-car garage for a neighbor—then built his first house in Queens, one year after graduating from high school. From these modest beginnings, Fred Trump built a successful company which in his son's words was "classic Horatio Alger."

AMBITION

Donald grew up in a traditional family with his four siblings and from the time he could walk, would often accompany his father on construction rounds. As a teen, he began to get more involved, watching his father negotiate prices on everything from maintenance supplies to property.

The lessons stuck. With a clear sense of ambition, Donald Trump propelled his early interest in his father's business into his present role as America's most famous entrepreneur and business tycoon.

SOURCE:
Trump—The Art of the Deal, Donald J. Trump with Tony Schwartz (Random House, New York, 1987).

FAMOUS CHILD:	**Dean Martin (Dino Crocetti, then Dino Martini)**
FATHER'S NAME:	**Guy Crocetti (Gaetano Crocetti)**
PAPA SAID:	*"Nice country, America."*

Big stars fought for tables up front—Clark Gable, Fred Astaire, Humphrey Bogart, Gene Kelly, Gary Cooper, and others. According to comedian Jerry Lewis, "It was incredible." The scene? Slapsy Maxie's Cafe in Los Angeles in 1948. Coming off successful television appearances on Ed Sullivan's *Toast of the Town* and Milton Berle's *Texaco Star Theater*, Dean Martin and Jerry Lewis were opening on the West Coast. Gaetano and Angelina Crocetti, as guests of their son, Dean Martin, were right up front, proudly watching the commotion. Author Nick Tosches relates, "As Gaetano looked around, he found himself slowly nodding in vague confirmation, saying words that had passed through his lips countless times before, at one time or the other bearing every tone in irony's spectrum: 'Nice country, America.' "

From the Abruzzi region of Italy, through Ellis Island, to the steel town of Steubenville, Ohio, nineteen-year-old Gaetano Crocetti traveled and went from a farm laborer who could barely read or write to a barber who always earned a decent living for his family. "A good *barbière*," Gaetano said, "was his own man." And now the reward—a son at the top in show business!

Young Dino Crocetti enjoyed a happy childhood, relating that he "never had to peddle newspapers" because his father was a successful barber. Most of his early years were spent playing cowboys and viewing hero Tom Mix at the Saturday matinees. He always sang around the house, deciding at an early age that he wanted to be an entertainer. For a time he tried boxing, but of twelve fights, Dino relates, "I won all but eleven of them."

With the onset of the Depression, Dino, according to Tosches, "began to surmise that life was a racket with which morality had little to do." Soon he was gambling in "alley games" with older boys, dealing blackjacks and working craps while explaining to his concerned parents, "I'm not a gambler. I deal; I work." Dino never had a police record, however, and began to love the fancy clothes, glitz, and glamour of the entertainment side of the business instead.

Now, Dino knew where his life was taking him. He studied every song that Bing Crosby sang in the movies and soon had his first singing job, in Cleveland for "$35 a week, a free room, and a fifty percent discount on food." With an ambition similar to his dad's, Dean Martin's career soared as he quickly became one of the most popular entertainers of his era.

SOURCE:
Dino, Nick Tosches (Doubleday, New York, 1992).

Famous Child:	F. Scott Fitzgerald
Father's Name:	Edward Fitzgerald

Papa Wrote: *"My dear Scott:*

"I enclose $1.00. Spend it liberally, generously, carefully, judiciously, sensibly. Get from it pleasure, wisdom, health, and experience."

orn shortly after the deaths of two of his older siblings, Scott was forever doted upon. Reminiscing as an adult, he said, "I think I started then to be a writer." Named for Francis Scott Key, who wrote *The Star-Spangled Banner* and who was a second cousin three times removed, Francis Scott Fitzgerald's name was a constant reminder of his connection to an ambitious relative who had attained significant fame and success.

But then, the Fitzgerald home in St. Paul, Minnesota—just around the corner from railroad magnate James J. Hill's palatial estate—was a reminder that, although Edward Fitzgerald owned his own business, the family never quite fit into St. Paul's upper class. F. Scott was always fascinated with James Hill and the society he represented. Twelve-year-old Scott received his dad's one dollar and poignant advice while at summer camp in Frontenac, Minnesota. Money, later a symbol of both the father's and son's ambition, would forever haunt them both.

Edward Fitzgerald struggled. His business struggled. Finally, he lost the business, and the family moved to Buffalo, New York, for his job as a grocery salesman. Edward finally lost even this job when F. Scott was eleven, devastating the entire family.

F. Scott Fitzgerald took up the pen. Throughout his writing are common threads: fame, money, success, and the everyday lives of those in high society played against the tragic stories of those to whom fame, money, and success would never come. At the height of his own success as a writer, F. Scott Fitzgerald "felt guilty because he did not deserve these blessings," according to author Jeffrey Meyers.

The Great Gatsby and *Tender Is the Night* both deal with the themes of ambition, success, and failure that his dad had experienced many years before. In an essay, "The Death of My Father," Fitzgerald writes, "I loved my father—always deep in my subconscious I have referred judgments back to him, what he would have thought or done." Speaking of his father later in life, F. Scott Fitzgerald added, "He came from tired old stock with very little left of vitality and mental energy, but he managed to raise a little for me."

SOURCES:

Scott Fitzgerald—A Biography, Jeffrey Meyers (HarperCollins, New York, 1994).

Some Sort of Epic Grandeur—The Life of F. Scott Fitzgerald, Matthew J. Bruccoli (Harcourt Brace Jovanovich, New York, 1981).

FAMOUS CHILD:	Monica Seles
FATHER'S NAME:	Karolj Seles

PAPA SAID: *"If you want to achieve something great in anything, you have to like what you do, work long and hard, and sweat a lot to reach your goal."*

Whatever Karolj Seles began hitting tennis balls to his five-year-old daughter, Monica, he was impressed with her native ability but tolerant enough to accept her "resignation" two weeks later. He went on practicing with her thirteen-year-old brother, Zoltan. Two years later, perhaps inspired by her brother's success or jealous of it, seven-year-old Monica realized that tennis might be fun after all.

That was part of Karolj's plan—make it fun. As an award-winning illustrator, he used cartoons and stuffed animals on the court to keep tennis fun for his young daughter. He avoided the pressure by keeping her away from real tennis courts at first, and by having her hit balls over a rope tied between two cars in a parking lot. Seles' biographer, Joe Layden, notes that Karolj, "understood intuitively what so many coaches either ignore or forget: the importance of having fun."

Her speed and power quickly brought Monica considerable attention when at nine she won the 1983 Yugoslavian twelve-and-under championship, and over the next two years won similar events in Europe and at the Miami Orange Bowl. Her efforts at the Orange Bowl brought her to the attention of tennis instructor Nick Bollettieri, who encouraged Karolj to send Monica, chaperoned by her twenty-one-year-old brother Zoltan, to his Tennis Academy in Miami the next year so she could play tennis year-round.

After six months she was joined by her parents. The formal relationship with Bollettieri ended in 1990 as her success bloomed and her father resumed his role as her primary coach. After some shocking wins over older players, Monica continued her ascendance into the tennis hierarchy and at fourteen was ranked among the top players. That ranking brought with it the intense jealousy of a fan of one of her rivals, and in 1993 the tennis world was shocked by her stabbing at an event in Hamburg, Germany. For the next two years, Monica sought to regain her physical and psychological strength.

Monica Seles showed the world she had come back when she advanced to the finals of the 1995 U.S. Open. And she continues to be one of the top players in tennis.

SOURCE:
Return of a Champion—The Monica Seles Story, Joe Layden (St. Martin's Press, New York, 1996).

FAMOUS CHILD:	Charles Dickens
FATHER'S NAME:	John Dickens

PAPA SAID: *"If you were to be persevering and were to work hard, you might someday come to live in it."*

*J*ohn Dickens spoke these words as he walked with his son past the imposing mansion, Gad's Hill Place, outside Rochester, England. Young Charles stopped, and stood in admiration. Thirty-six years later, Charles Dickens bought the house. Author Peter Ackroyd explains, "Without a doubt, a man heavily influenced by his father's praise would spend the next thirty years of his life trying to earn it."

John Dickens, whose mother was a servant and whose grandparents worked as a butler and a housekeeper, lived in the midst of splendor until he was twenty-one. As such, author Ackroyd adds, "He believed all his life that he would be sheltered." After the age of twenty-one, when he was on his own, it just didn't happen.

Charles Dickens, describing himself as "a very odd little child with the first faint shadows of all my books in my head," grew up moving from town to town as the fortunes of his father's work in the Naval Pay Office ebbed and flowed. He watched as his father was taken to debtors' prison, hearing him say as he left that the sun had set on him forever. These words, spoken in 1824, "broke my heart," Charles would say later, and propelled the twelve-year-old into jobs with ten-hour days. The seeds of his ambition were sown.

The observant child watched and remembered many of the characters in his neighborhoods, re-creating them in his fiction later. Few of these characters, however, were as well documented or as often re-created as those characters based on his father, John Dickens. In a complicated relationship that thrived on highs and lows, Charles Dickens reinvented his father in his fiction, while mimicking his words and rhythm of speech. Ironically, though tormented by his father's inability to control his finances, he delighted in living in lower-class neighborhoods in bustling towns. The people who lived in such places were earthy, wore old, loose-fitting clothes, and gave color to the tales he told.

Over a long literary career, the Victorian novelist had created almost two thousand characters. In 1870, at the age of fifty-eight, he was buried in Westminster Abbey. After the funeral, Charles' son found several small bouquets of flowers tied up with pieces of rag. Dickens, who had described his characters with such compassion after having witnessed the heartbreaking financial struggles of his father, would have appreciated the anonymous gift.

SOURCE:
Dickens, Peter Ackroyd (HarperCollins Publishers, New York, 1990).

FAMOUS CHILD:	Emily Post
FATHER'S NAME:	Bruce Price

PAPA SAID: *"From the instant we are born we start building—bodies, minds, characters, friendships, careers, fortunes, reputations. Living is building. If you know the laws and respect them, you can't help building well."*

To prominent architect Bruce Price, understanding life in terms of construction made a lot of sense. To his daughter, Emily, who had just asked in exasperation, "Darling Papa, don't you ever think of anything but architecture?" the answer was filled with both meaning and prophesy.

Emily Price grew up with the help of governesses in a distinguished family, attending private schools in New York and Baltimore, then married Edwin Post, son of a prominent Long Island family, and gave birth to two boys. Life in New York's Washington Square was fairly uncomplicated until she found herself divorced and with a lifestyle to support. Emily picked up a pen and began to write.

Happy with her newfound talent, Emily spent mornings writing, while refusing social invitations and resenting interruptions. When she was discouraged, her father urged her on, explaining that the two of them were a lot alike. "We are only fully ourselves when we are working. And when we are not working, we are miserable, whether we realize it or not."

Magazines published several of her stories of American and European high society and others appeared in book form, and later she toured Europe as a "traveling correspondent" in the months before World War I. Once her book *Etiquette, The Blue Book of Social Usage* appeared, she never had to worry about maintaining her position in society. The seven-hundred-page bestseller became the last word on the subject of social behavior to a society determined to do things right.

Years later, Emily Post accompanied her ailing father to France, where he planned to sketch and where there were many things he wanted to see. He died there, but Bruce Price's advice lives on—in his daughter's book of etiquette.

SOURCE:
Truly Emily Post, Edwin Post (Funk and Wagnalls, New York, 1961).

FAMOUS CHILD:	Miles Dewey Davis III
FATHER'S NAME:	Miles Dewey Davis II

PAPA SAID: *"By genetics and breeding Miles is always going to be ahead of his time. Historically way back into slavery days, the Davises have been musicians and performed classical works in the homes of the plantation owners."*

*J*azz trumpet immortal Miles Davis a violinist? He might have been one if his mother had won out. She wanted him to play the violin and go to Fisk University in Nashville to major in music. Instead, his father bought him a trumpet and enrolled him at the Juilliard School of Music in New York.

While music was in his family's slave tradition, after the emancipation his accountant-trained grandfather decided that Miles' father would not be allowed to play music because "the only place a Negro could play then was in barrelhouses [clip joints or brothels]." His father instead went to dental school and started a successful practice in St. Louis.

Miles' father could afford to buy him both a trumpet and private lessons and introduced him to one of his dental patients, jazz trumpet teacher Elwood Buchanan. Elwood taught Miles how to read music and introduced him to his professional mentor, trumpet star Clark Terry. Guided by Terry, Miles performed regularly in high school and received offers to join various bands.

While in New York at Juilliard, young Davis decided that he could learn more in the jazz clubs along Fifty-second Street, and he dropped out of school. He quickly made a name for himself playing with Dizzy Gillespie and Charlie Parker. In spite of his success, Miles struggled with depression and a four-year drug habit, but by 1951 he had won the battle. Miles' father proudly commented, "It had to put a hard crust on Miles. He had an iron will that broke it and the willpower applied to everything he did as a result. I'm proud of him."

With his drug habit behind him, Davis became a major player on the jazz scene. He led the development of a new jazz form called bebop and became known as "The Phoenix" because of his ability to regenerate his creative urge. He also was known as a bandleader who discovered and developed a long list of jazz giants, such as John Coltrane and Herbie Hancock.

SOURCES:
Miles Davis: A Biography, by Ian Carr (William Morrow, New York, 1982).
Miles Davis: A Musical Biography, Bill Cole (William Morrow, New York, 1974).

FAMOUS CHILD: A. J. Foyt Jr. (Anthony Joseph)

FATHER'S NAME: A. J. Foyt Sr. (Anthony Joseph)

PAPA SAID: *"I guess you're gonna be a race driver, A. J. Well, you gotta promise me one thing: Always drive good equipment. If you're not gonna drive the best race cars in the best shape, then don't even bother."*

T he famous race car driver who won a record four Indianapolis 500 races got an early start as the son and grandson of mechanics. He recalls that one of his early motivations was hearing other drivers ridicule his less-than-successful father with comments like, "Whatsamatter, kid, can't your daddy build race cars?" His father did, however, build three-year-old A. J. Junior his own race car. By the time his son was five, A. J. Senior had arranged that he race another driver. Young A. J. won, and the family's racing fortunes were about to change.

Foyt recalls "wanting to be a race driver" among his earliest memories. By the time he was fifteen, he notes, "There was not much I didn't know about building and tuning race cars." His dream was to race at the Mecca of racing—Indianapolis. In describing the route from Texas to Indianapolis, Foyt points out that while the route on the map is well defined, for a racer in the 1950s it meant being the absolute best at your local track and slowly moving up the various levels of the racing hierarchy. He worked for his father and looked for every opportunity to race. Every week, his dad and he would leave their Houston home and go to San Antonio for a race.

He won an Indianapolis 500 race in 1961, and by 1977 had become the first to ever win four. A. J. Senior was with him through the wins, losses, and occasional major accidents. While A. J. was writing his autobiography in 1983, his father was diagnosed with cancer. He wrote, "I really don't know how to handle it. I've never been in auto racing without Daddy. I haven't got to the point where I can be philosophical about it."

SOURCE:
A.J.—The Life of America's Greatest Race Car Driver, A. J. Foyt with William Neely (New York Times Book Company, New York, 1983).

FAMOUS CHILD:	Mary Cassatt
FATHER'S NAME:	Robert S. Cassatt
PAPA SAID:	*"I would almost rather see you dead."*

ary Cassatt was twenty-one when her father said this to her. Born in 1845, she spent four years as a child with her family in Italy and France and was exposed to and fascinated by the great masters. Her wealthy father, always pleased with her love of art, then sent her to the Pennsylvania Academy of the Fine Arts in Philadelphia. After all, many prominent Victorian young ladies enjoyed the hobby of painting lovely pictures. When his daughter decided to make art her career, however, Robert S. Cassatt was extremely disappointed. According to author Robin McKown, "Like many of his class, he admired art as culture but felt that artists were not quite respectable. The idea of the daughter of a gentleman painting for a living was distinctly shocking to him."

In an era when women artists were not taken seriously, Mary Cassatt achieved great respect during her own lifetime not only among her fellow Impressionists, but also among art lovers throughout Europe and America. Although many of her pieces were selected for display at the more conservative juried shows in Paris, where she and her family lived, she always loved her forays into the less conventional art form, Impressionism. And, inspired by her friends and fellow artists Edgar Degas, Claude Monet, and Édouard Manet, she excelled at it.

Mary Cassatt supported herself throughout her long career, leaving more than 225 prints and 940 paintings in museums and homes all over the world. Despite his initial resistance, Robert Cassatt who was immortalized in his daughter's painting *Mr. Robert S. Cassatt on Horseback*, very soon recognized her great talent, and proudly sent newspaper clippings and reviews of her shows to their relatives.

SOURCES:
Mary Cassatt, Susan E. Meyer (Harry N. Abrams, New York, 1990).
The World of Mary Cassatt, Robin McKown (Thomas Y. Crowell, New York, 1972).

COURAGE

John Wayne
Judy Collins
Joan Baez
John Brown
Clarence Darrow
Vladimir Horowitz
Dr. Ruth Westheimer
Pete Seeger
Beverly Sills
Norman Schwarzkopf
Harriet Beecher Stowe
Christopher Reeve

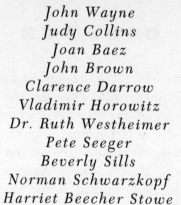

COURAGE

*S*idney Smith said, "A great deal of talent is lost in this world for the want of a little courage." In many of our stories, a father's demonstration of courage has led to a child's use of it during times of challenge.

Stories of courage frequently develop out of devastating life events, such as war, depression, or extreme poverty. Norman Schwarzkopf Sr. handed Norman Junior his West Point sword before he went off to war, while declaring his son the "head of the house." Seven-year-old Norman listened carefully, assumed increasing responsibilities, and lived to lead as a general in his own military career. Young Karola Ruth Siegel has always treasured her father's letters from a concentration camp. After his death she courageously carried on with his "love of life and learning" to become Dr. Ruth Westheimer, a prominent doctor who counsels and advises millions.

By demonstrating political courage, fathers frequently pass on to their children a similar legacy. Owen Brown talked of God's creatures being equal whether they were white, red, or black. His son, John, listened carefully and by the time he was an adult, he had publicly dedicated his life to abolishing slavery. Sharing his father's convictions, John Brown supported a political mission that eventually led not only to his death but to the onset of the Civil War.

A toddler named Pete danced along as his wealthy and musical father, Charles Seeger, fulfilled his mission to bring music to the poor of the South. Young Joan listened as her father, Dr. Albert Baez, explained his refusal to work in the defense industry as a research physicist. As adults, Pete Seeger and Joan Baez sang protest songs and courageously led America's struggle of conscience during the Vietnam War.

Most of us are inspired by those who demonstrate moral courage in the face of debilitating handicaps. Millions watched in 1996 as Christopher Reeve addressed the Democratic convention from a wheelchair. His father had written of the plight of migrant farm workers years earlier, providing a foundation for his son's own commitment to worthwhile causes. This time, however, Reeve's cause was a personal one—the plea for research money to find a cure for his spinal injury. Judy watched her blind father, Charles Collins, struggle to live an ordinary life and accomplish extraordinary things. Witnessing his courage made it easier for her to summon her own later on, when she picked up her guitar and sang songs of protest in the 1960s.

FATHER KNEW BEST

A father's demonstration of courage is often quiet and unspoken, the message subtle but enduring. The courage may have been a result of a devastating life event, political conflict, or personal challenge. When times got tough, however, the child knew what to do.

FAMOUS CHILD:	John Wayne
	(Marion Michael Morrison)
FATHER'S NAME:	Clyde Morrison

PAPA SAID: *"Mind you, don't go looking for fights, but if you find yourself in one, make damn sure you win."*

arion Michael Morrison's father, Clyde, came from a long line of "farmers who subscribed to the American work ethic," according to John Wayne's widow, author Pilar Wayne. He spent most of his adult life, however, trying to avoid farming. After time spent at the University of Iowa, he became a pharmacist's clerk, saved money for a down payment on a pharmacy in Earlham, Iowa, and provided well for his family of a wife and two sons—Marion was the older by five years. Clyde, a charming, handsome man of medium height, praised his young son for his bravery and always advised him not to run from a fight.

Born in Winterset, Iowa, in 1907 with the name Marion and of slight stature in his early years, John Wayne found himself with many battles to fight, prompting his dad's advice. Although a dreamer and a poor money manager, Clyde Morrison was a man of principle, and felt that one must "never insult another on purpose and never break his given word." Widow Pilar Wayne added, "Duke loved his father with a quiet and steady affection. He absorbed his teachings and made them part of his own character."

In 1915, when a bout with tuberculosis led him to seek out a hot, dry climate, Clyde moved his family to an eighty-acre ranch in California on the edge of the Mojave Desert, where young Marion learned to ride horses and to absorb the culture of the West. The unyielding desert soil, however, would not grow crops, so when Clyde felt better a year later, the family moved to Glendale, California, where at the age of eleven Marion Morrison got a job delivering newspapers with his little dog, Duke. Local firemen watched the two go by every day and referred to them as "Little Duke" and "Big Duke." Henceforth, "Duke," later known as John Wayne (and relieved to put the name "Marion" to rest), felt better about himself. He went on to play high school football and to win a football scholarship to the University of Southern California.

John Wayne starred in over 150 movies, most based on stories of the Western frontier. Years later, he said, "A man's got to have a code, a creed to live by, no matter what his job." The characters he portrayed were strong, brave, and courageous, much the same attributes instilled in him by his father, Clyde Morrison, so many years before.

SOURCE:
John Wayne—My Life with the Duke, Pilar Wayne with Alex Thorleifson (McGraw-Hill, New York, 1987).

FAMOUS CHILD: Judy Collins

FATHER'S NAME: Charles Thomas Collins

PAPA SAID: *"People say of me that I must be reconciled to my physical condition. That is, of course, ridiculous. To be reconciled is merely to sit passively on your jail bunk, weary of kicking at the interlaced ironwork in front of you. I am not reconciled to anything."*

harles Collins, a handsome, optimistic Irishman from a musical farming family, was born in Nez Perce, Idaho, a former Indian reservation. As a child, he gradually lost his sight, becoming legally blind at the age of four. At seven, he was admitted to an institution for the handicapped, where he was taught piano tuning and weaving. The courageous and energetic youngster, however, "refused to let his handicap define him," according to Judy, and quickly learned to navigate without the use of a cane or Seeing Eye dog. "He walked tall and straight, with his shoulders thrown back, head held high. He called the sound of his shoes on the street his 'radar,'" Judy related. "The sound of his footsteps told him where he was going and gave him a greater-than-human presence."

Not content to limit himself to a confining career defined by his handicap, he graduated from public high school in Boise and the University of Idaho, started a dance band, and had his own radio show where he sang with his clear Irish tenor voice. Judy, who had spent her entire childhood singing, playing the piano, and harmonizing with him, appeared on the program and toured with him throughout the upper northwestern states. "This tyke," Charles often said, "can harmonize with anything, even a car horn or a train whistle."

Ultimately it was not only through music, but also through a sequence of serious health problems, that Judy's relationship with her father continued to strengthen. At the age of ten, having contracted polio before Dr. Salk invented the vaccine, Judy spent one month isolated from her family, then another recuperating in the hospital. It was the memory of her father's sitting by her bed late one night after her return home from the hospital, his face turned toward her, which inspired the song "My Father" that Judy Collins composed and sang many years later. She recalled that she saw "a curiously tranquil look on his face. I felt a sense of peace from him there in the dimly lit room."

When he died suddenly in 1968, Judy recalled, "He was so tough, so delicate, so musical, so much of an enigma to me, and so indelible on my own life." Mustering a courage and tenacity modeled by her father, Judy became involved in the Vietnam War protest movement and was arrested on the steps of the Capitol Building in Washington, D.C., in 1971. The folksinger concluded her autobiography: "There is nothing in the promise that says the bird that flies out of the ashes will always fly a perfect course; only that she will rise from the ashes on new wings."

SOURCE:
Judy Collins—Trust Your Heart, Judy Collins (Houghton Mifflin, Boston, 1987).

FAMOUS CHILD: Joan Chandos Baez

FATHER'S NAME: Albert Baez

PAPA SAID: *"Well, honey, it's a good cause, and a day worth remembering."*

Joan Baez's father, Albert, emigrated at the age of two from Puebla, Mexico, to Brooklyn. Although he spent his childhood wanting to be a minister and even preached at the age of nineteen in his father's church, his love of "anything mechanical" soon took precedence, as he worked up from an interest in crystal radios to the intricacies of mathematics and then physics. Albert worked his way through school, earning both a master's degree and a doctorate at Stanford. He accepted a position as research physicist at Cornell University in New York, where he became increasingly disturbed by his work in the defense industry. This struggle of conscience and courage led him both to the Quaker religion and to a heartfelt pacifism, as he began to steer his career toward teaching at the college level.

After the family moved due to her father's new job at MIT (Massachusetts Institute of Technology), Joan immersed herself in Harvard Square's bookstores and coffee houses while learning to play the guitar. Soon her voice could be heard not only along the banks of the Charles River, but also in the local coffee houses.

At a conference on world issues presented by the Quakers, a teenage Joan Baez heard a twenty-seven-year-old preacher named Martin Luther King Jr. speak. In Joan's words, "King gave a shape and a name to my passionate but ill-articulated beliefs." With a social and political courage modeled by her father years before, and augmented by King's compelling message of civil rights, Baez went on to sing her own message of peace and protest to a country struggling in the sixties and seventies with issues surrounding both civil rights and the antiwar movement.

Years later, in 1985, Joan Baez performed with entertainers in both London and Philadelphia in a ten-hour nationally televised benefit for famine victims—Live Aid, watched by 1.5 billion people throughout the world. In the middle of the concert a proud but modest Joan Baez called home to speak to her equally proud parents and ask them if she should take part in the finale. Both parents answered in the affirmative, as Albert Baez referred to the memorable event as "a good cause, and a day worth remembering. They need more of you, honey." Joan hung up and went back up to the stage.

Joan lovingly describes her dad as "a short, handsome Mexican scientist who still attends Quaker meetings, thinks globally, and is preoccupied with the betterment of all people." "Decency," Joan adds, "would be his legacy to us."

SOURCE:
Joan Baez—And a Voice to Sing With, Joan Baez (Summit Books, New York, 1987).

FAMOUS CHILD: John Brown

FATHER'S NAME: Owen Brown

PAPA SAID: *"I perceive that God is no respecter of persons. Be they white or red, or even black, they're all God's creatures, and the white man's got no right to rob them or to make slaves of them. And if we do, then they got every right to fight back at us."*

Cobbler Owen Brown was always clear in his dislike of slavery—having strongly supported a Connecticut law to end the practice in 1784. As his trade became less and less profitable, Owen was forced to relocate his family by wagon train to Ohio, where Indians outnumbered the settlers, causing significant anxiety. A pioneer along the trail, having heard of Indian attacks and massacres, approached Owen with the opinion that the settlers had a right to take over, for the Indians didn't have title to the land and didn't farm or build cities. Five-year-old John Brown never forgot his father's courageous words in response.

As a child, John loved the outdoors, preferred working with

his father to attending school, and spent hours reading about history. As he approached adulthood, John Brown supported the antislavery movement, much as his father had. After John had witnessed the abuse of a slave, then heard of the death of a newspaper publisher by a pro-slavery mob in 1837, he declared at a meeting in Ohio, "Here, before God, in the presence of these witnesses, from this time, I consecrate my life to the destruction of slavery."

In his efforts, John Brown traveled throughout the country, made speeches, and mustered an army of fighting men while working to support the "underground railroad," which provided slaves a means of escape. John Brown's "master plan" included supporting a large movement of "runaways" led and protected by his army, and attacking Harpers Ferry, West Virginia, where large numbers of arms were stored. This attack on Harpers Ferry in 1859 resulted both in the death of two of his sons and his well-publicized trial for treason, after which he was sentenced to death by hanging.

Although captured by the United States Marines and declared guilty of treason by the United States government, John Brown's courageous efforts were lauded by many. Ralph Waldo Emerson compared the importance of a speech he gave in the courtroom with Lincoln's Gettysburg Address. John Brown was hung in Virginia in 1859, firmly establishing his legend.

Only two years later, the Civil War began over the same issue of slavery. As the soldiers marched in step to war, many were heard singing a song about John Brown's body lying in a grave while his soul went marching on.

SOURCE:
John Brown—A Cry for Freedom, Lorenz Graham (Thomas Y. Crowell, New York, 1980).

FAMOUS CHILD:	Clarence Seward Darrow
FATHER'S NAME:	Amirus Darrow

PAPA... *told stories of an "advance army of reformers, black and white, who went up and down the land arousing the dulled conscience of the people to a sense of justice to the slave. They used to make my father's home their stopping place, and any sort of vacant room was the forum where they told of the black man's wrongs."*

larence Darrow, born in 1857, witnessed as a young child many of the events surrounding the Civil War close at hand. The area of Kinsman, Ohio, a major stop in the underground railroad, was full of people supportive of the abolitionist cause. Many would stop at the Darrow home, where the courageous Amirus Darrow made them welcome while providing a forum for their views. Union soldiers marched past the house on the way to southern skirmishes, and, as the Civil War progressed, Amirus struggled to earn a living by making caskets and building furniture in the small town of four hundred people.

Clarence said that his father was "an impractical man whose

extraordinary devotion to learning left him little time to earn a living." The house was full of books—on chairs, tables, shelves, and the floor—and all of the children were taught to love them. A fan of the classics and well-read in the disciplines of philosophy, history, and theology, Amirus developed a personal philosophy that often went against prevailing beliefs. "My father was the village infidel and gradually came to glory in his reputation," Clarence noted. Author Kevin Tierney explains, "He played this role with such adeptness that his son would seek to emulate it throughout his life, magnifying it to a national career."

Although he loved to read, Clarence rejected the classical studies his father embraced and never was a diligent student, describing formal education as an "appalling waste of time." Relieved to leave Allegheny College at the end of his freshman year in order to save his father money during a depression, Clarence continued to read voraciously, while remembering most everything he ever read. Once he decided that law would be his avocation, he studied independently without attending law school, and passed the bar. As a country lawyer, he refused to "argue cases in which he didn't believe," according to Tierney.

Clarence Darrow, a legend throughout his long and courageous career, remained an idealist, independent thinker, writer, reformist, lawyer, and intellectual, although possessing little formal education. The show business newspaper *Variety* described him as "America's greatest one-man stage draw" after his highly publicized role as defense attorney in the 1925 Scopes trial, which concerned evolution. His courtroom experiences were the subject of the popular theater and film productions *Compulsion* and *Inherit the Wind*.

SOURCE:
Darrow—A Biography, Kevin Tierney (Thomas Y. Crowell, New York, 1979).

FAMOUS CHILD:	Vladimir Horowitz
FATHER'S NAME:	Samuel Horowitz
PAPA SAID:	*"That boy will be a famous pianist."*

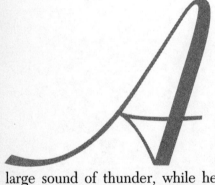

t the age of six, young Vladimir Horowitz sat down at the piano. His small hands made the large sound of thunder, while he recited a story to add verbal color to the sound. His father, Samuel Horowitz, listened in the next room and made this accurate prediction.

Samuel Horowitz, an electrical engineer who worked for both American and Russian firms in Russia, was a cultured man who read Dickens and Dumas, appreciated good music, and with his wife raised a family of four children in the Ukraine. All the children took piano, but Vladimir stood out from the rest, composing his first pieces at the age of eight. By the age of thirteen, Vladimir had entered the Kiev Conservatory.

By the 1920s, however, all that Kiev had to offer culturally was challenged by war and chaos. During the reign of terror and revolution, Samuel Horowitz lost his business, his apartment, and all the money the family had been able to save, while Vladimir was forced to perform concerts to keep food on the table. In spite of their loss, the courageous family was well represented at Vladimir's first public concert in Kiev—just before he emigrated to Berlin in the midst of the conflict.

Vladimir sent money home regularly, and later Samuel accompanied his son on a short concert tour through Western Europe. After returning home to Russia, however, Samuel Horowitz was arrested during a Stalinist purge, sentenced to prison, and died there soon after. The devastated young pianist left his homeland, refused to return for sixty-one years, and was haunted throughout his life by his memories and, perhaps as a result, by frequent and extreme stage fright.

In 1986, an eighty-three-year-old Vladimir Horowitz returned to Russia to perform at the Great Hall of the Moscow Conservatory. The hall was filled with enthusiastic Russian citizens and press from around the world. Showing a courage modeled by his father years earlier, Vladimir conquered his stage fright and performed the concert of his life. He died, several years later, just before the staggering political upheaval of 1989–1991 that restored Leningrad once again to St. Petersburg.

SOURCE:
Horowitz—His Life and Music, Harold C. Schonberg (Simon & Schuster, New York, 1992).

FAMOUS CHILD:	Dr. Ruth Westheimer
	(Karola Ruth Siegel)
FATHER'S NAME:	Julius Siegel

PAPA WROTE: *"Dear Karola!*

On the New Year I congratulate you.
May you remain hearty.
Many of your wishes should be fulfilled
To be a good girl.
And mainly I wish that you should continue
To write in a happy mood.
And always have goodwill.
Then you are going to be content on this earth."

It was the Jewish New Year in September 1941. Julius Siegel, just out of detention camp, picked up a pen to write to his daughter, Karola Ruth, who was living in a Swiss orphanage. She and three hundred other German-Jewish children had been taken in a "Kinder transport" to avoid the tumultuous events in Germany. As a German Jew, a child under sixteen with a father in concentration camp, she qualified for the transport—one of only 300 children who did, out of a population of 550,000. It was a stroke of luck—a promise of life. She never saw her parents again, and remained in Switzerland six years. Her courageous and devoted father did not know it then, but this would be his last letter—and one that his daughter would cherish always.

Karola Ruth had lived happily in a four-room row house with her father, mother, and grandmother in Frankfurt. Then had come Kristallnacht. On November 9, 1938, life as ten-year-old Karola knew it ended. Synagogues were burned. Schools were closed. Jews were killed. Businesses were destroyed. That's when Karola Ruth started sleeping in her parents' bed. Within a week, there was a knock at the door and "several intimidating men" took her father away.

After Kristallnacht, Julius Siegel spent evenings writing his daughter poems and letters. Once out of detention camp, he tried to emigrate, an almost impossible task, and eventually was deported to a Polish ghetto with his wife and mother-in-law—a first step to another concentration camp. Karola Ruth never heard from her family again.

At seventeen, Karola Ruth emigrated to Israel, then France, and finally the United States, where she qualified for a scholarship, as a Nazi survivor, to the New School for Social Research in New York. Possessing the courage of her father, she never looked back, but looked ahead, in her father's words, "with good-will." Now a media personality, author, and one of America's most famous psychosexual therapists, Dr. Ruth credits her father, Julius Siegel, with giving her a wonderful gift: "a love of and a joy in learning."

SOURCE:
Dr. Ruth Westheimer—All in a Lifetime, Dr. Ruth Westheimer with Ben Yagoda (Warner Books, New York, 1987).

FAMOUS CHILD: Pete Seeger

FATHER'S NAME: Charles Seeger

PAPA SAID: *"I staked everything that we had on that trip—to bring music to the poor people of America, who didn't have any music."*

harles Seeger was surrounded by good fortune. He grew up on the family estate on Staten Island, the son of an old and well-connected Yankee family. He studied music at Harvard and mastered several musical instruments. He was a full professor at the University of California at Berkeley—the youngest full professor in the history of the school.

Then he met the young economist Carleton Parker. Carleton described the plight of the migrant farmworkers in the San Joaquin Valley and took Charles to see the community firsthand. Charles Seeger was never the same. With a growing focus on "those less fortunate" and toward organizing the IWW (Industrial Workers of the World), this World War I conscientious objector became more and more disillusioned with academia. After announcing his intentions to his conservative family and academic peers, Charles resigned from the university, left with his wife and two sons for New Jersey, and moved into his parents' estate near the Hudson River. In 1919 a third son, Pete, was born. Soon after, Charles Seeger decided to set out with his young family on a journey to bring music to the rural poor.

From a toddler who danced and sang to his father's music in the mountains of the South, Pete Seeger went on to attend Harvard. He left as a sophomore, however, to "hobo" across the country while playing and writing music. He hitchhiked across the country with Woody Guthrie and was called a "saint" by Bob Dylan. He has sung his folk songs of protest to fans in over forty countries—often challenging governments, which generally don't agree with his views—and was blacklisted by the United States government in the fifties. He was invited to march from Selma to Montgomery at the personal invitation of Dr. Martin Luther King. Today, he lives along the Hudson River and fights against its pollution. The author of the songs "If I Had a Hammer" and "Where Have All the Flowers Gone?" has more than fifty albums to his name.

With a courage initiated by his father many years before, Pete Seeger sings and plays to bigger and bigger audiences. Pete Seeger calls his father "the one person that all my life I was able to talk and argue with." According to author David King Dunaway, Pete Seeger associated folk music with a "lifestyle uncomplicated by materialism" and it was "his window into rural life in America"—the same rural America that his father had showed him many years before.

SOURCE:
How Can I Keep from Singing: Pete Seeger, David King Dunaway (McGraw-Hill, New York, 1981).

FAMOUS CHILD:	Beverly Sills (Belle Silverman)
FATHER'S NAME:	Morris Silverman

PAPA SAID: *"You must never feel that there is no way out of a situation that makes you unhappy."*

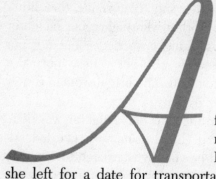

fter saying this, Morris Silverman handed his daughter, Belle, a twenty-dollar bill as she left for a date for transportation home in case she wasn't having a good time. The advice, however, "took on a lot of other forms later on," writes Beverly, and symbolized for her the freedom to choose while allowing her to deal positively with events over which she had no control.

Beverly Sills' career and personal life sparkle with the threads of courage that her father's message instilled. She summoned this courage at the end of a long performing career to accept the role of general director of the same opera company with which she sang—the first "diva" to hold this position. She has labored tirelessly to bring the company out of its financial difficulties, approaching each problem with a positive attitude.

Although the affliction wasn't immediately apparent, Beverly's first child, a daughter named Muffy, was born deaf. With a positive attitude and the courage of her father, Beverly Sills explains, "Some people have commented on the irony of an opera singer's having a daughter who can't hear her sing. Believe me, that didn't enter the picture at all. I was a mother whose gorgeous daughter was deaf. My voice was the last thing I worried about her not being able to hear." Determined to raise her with as normal a life as possible, Beverly has succeeded. The bright woman is now a graphic artist and a joy to her parents.

A short six weeks after learning that her daughter was deaf, Beverly was told that her second child, a son, was retarded. Although devastated, Beverly and her family translated the tragedy into something positive and are active volunteers in an organization to prevent birth defects. "The way I did it," Beverly shares, "is to put on a happy face."

As a child, Belle Silverman was used to putting on a happy face. From a four-year-old who knew the words and notes to twenty-two arias, she turned into a seven-year-old who had a regular spot on *Major Bowes' Capitol Family Hour* on radio and was getting fan mail. For a traditional father who worked hard as the manager of an insurance company, this was amazing. By the time

COURAGE

Beverly Sills' career ended in a huge gala at the New York City Opera in October of 1980, she had performed for over thirty years in countries throughout the world.

SOURCE:
Beverly—An Autobiography, Beverly Sills and Lawrence Linderman (Bantam Books, New York, 1987).

FAMOUS CHILD:	General Norman Schwarzkopf Jr.
FATHER'S NAME:	Norman Schwarzkopf Sr.

PAPA SAID: *"Now, son, I'm depending on you. The responsibility is yours."*

With these words, Norman Schwarzkopf Sr. placed the Army saber he had received as a graduate of West Point in his seven-year-old namesake's hands. It was 1942, and the father was going off to war. West Point's motto, "Duty, Honor, Country," was his creed, and, the general adds, "it became mine."

Norman Senior grew up in a German-speaking family in Newark, graduating from West Point in time to serve first in World War I. At twenty-five, he was appointed by the governor of New Jersey to head up the state police—a position he held for fifteen years, and a challenging job at the time, for prohibition laws had resulted in legions of bootleggers, smugglers, and gangs throughout the state. During his reign in the 1930s, the state police investigated the highly publicized Lindbergh kidnapping case, which resulted in the execution of Bruno Hauptmann in 1936.

Norman Junior's childhood was dominated by everything military after his father gave him the saber—by his father's comings and goings; tales told by his father of World War II and Hitler; air raid drills and blackouts; the attack at Pearl Harbor; his father's meeting during the war with General George C. Marshall in Washington; pages and pages of his dad's letters to read—while having to struggle along with his mom and sisters alone.

By sixth grade, the lonesome young boy, in a houseful of girls, was thrilled to be going to a military school in the tradition of his father. After graduating from West Point, Norman Junior, by then an infantry second lieutenant, served two tours of duty in Vietnam and was decorated three times with the Silver Star, and returned a lieutenant colonel. After a series of promotions achieved during a variety of assignments, he received his fourth star as general in 1988. During the Persian Gulf War in 1991, as commander of a United States–led coalition of air, sea, and land forces, he achieved wide recognition and respect.

Referring to his father as "a selfless public servant, a true patriot, a man of honor, and a loving father," Norman Schwarz-kopf, though retired now, continues to proudly follow the West Point motto, "Duty, Honor, Country," much as his father did.

SOURCE:
General H. Norman Schwarzkopf—It Doesn't Take a Hero, Norman Schwarzkopf with Peter Motto (Bantam Books, New York, 1992).

FAMOUS CHILD: Harriet Beecher Stowe

FATHER'S NAME: Lyman Beecher

PAPA SAID: *"Oh, that this land would sink beneath its load of shame and misery . . ."*

Young Hattie sat in the Congregational meeting in Litchfield, Connecticut, and listened to her father's strong, eloquent words against slavery. "One day, years later," according to author Johanna Johnston, "when she had learned a good deal more about all kinds of slavery, she would cry out the same words." Minister Lyman Beecher, a prominent protester, preached eloquently against drinking, dueling, and slavery in the mid 1800s, from his churches in Connecticut, Boston, and then Cincinnati—a courageous stance at the time in a nation filled with political conflict.

After Lyman's move to Cincinnati to head up the Lane Seminary, when she was twenty-two, Harriet was exposed to events which later gave rise to her book *Uncle Tom's Cabin*. She joined a literary club there and met her husband, Calvin Stowe, while observing at closer range the issue of slavery. For the first time, she knew both free and slave blacks, observed the plights of runaways, and heard emotional debates on the issue, while living next to Kentucky, which was still a slave state.

As the mother of seven children, Harriet Beecher Stowe needed extra money, and using both her experience in Cincinnati and her father's sermons against slavery as inspiration, she wrote *Uncle Tom's Cabin* and quickly became a spokesman for northern abolitionists while achieving fame throughout the western world.

SOURCE:
Runaway to Heaven, Johanna Johnston (Doubleday, New York, 1963).

FAMOUS CHILD:	Christopher Reeve
FATHER'S NAME:	Franklin Reeve
PAPA SAID:	*"Ah, Jack Tanner, it's a great part, a great part."*

*F*ranklin Reeve was excited and ordered champagne. Christopher had just shared the news that he had the lead in *Superman*. Then it slowly dawned on Christopher: His dad thought that he had gotten the role of Jack Tanner in George Bernard Shaw's *Man and Superman*.

For Franklin Reeve, a graduate of Princeton with a Ph.D. from Columbia, popular culture was far, far away. He had loftier things on his mind—like translating Russian and Slavic literature and writing poetry. In the sixties, he had accompanied Robert Frost to Russia as an interpreter. Raised a child of privilege, he'd closed the door on both his family and their wealth and courageously made his own way, trading comfort for conviction. He was tough. He lived simply, and wrote a book about the plight of migrant farmworkers. For this man, Clark Kent was a stranger and academia was king.

Christopher grew up in a family shadowed by divorce. Franklin left when Christopher was three, but spent time with his son and taught him to sail. "He can do everything—from playing Parcheesi to translating Dostoyevsky," Chris shares. "I adore my father."

He spent his early years in Princeton, New Jersey. Having decided very young to be an actor, Chris had an Actor's Equity card by sixteen, then graduated from Cornell and took classes at Juilliard before acting in off-Broadway and Williamstown Theater productions. Then came *Superman*.

Chris lived a life as tough as those of Superman and his father, doing his own movie stunts while taking up daring hobbies like horse jumping. Then in 1995, during a competition in Virginia, he fell headfirst off his horse, breaking the top two vertebrae in his neck.

Now paralyzed, he has another role to play. After more than 150 plays, 17 movie roles, and a half dozen television movies, Chris faces life as a handicapped adult. For the man who spent a career supporting causes of all kind, from the Special Olympics to support for the arts, his most poignant philanthropy may lie ahead. In his speech to the Democratic National Convention in

1996, Christopher Reeve called for "breaking down the barriers in architecture and attitude" and supporting spinal injury research.

SOURCE:
Man of Steel—The Career and Courage of Christopher Reeve, Adrian Havill (Penguin, New York, 1996).

DEVOTION

Paul Simon
Jackie Kennedy Onassis
Bonnie Raitt
Luciano Pavarotti
Nichelle Nichols
Arthur Fiedler
Alexander Graham Bell
Cal Ripken Jr.
Pearl S. Buck
Johann Christian Bach
Selena
Woodrow Wilson
Candice Bergen
Pablo Picasso
Madame Curie
Eleanor Roosevelt
Liza Minnelli

DEVOTION

*E*nglish author Samuel Johnson said, "The most illiterate man who is touched with devotion, and uses frequent exercises of it, contracts a certain greatness of mind, mingled with a noble simplicity, that raises him above others of the same condition." And rich indeed are the children who have first experienced this devotion close to home—in the actions of their fathers.

Devoted fathers create a cushion of acceptance that a child carries for a lifetime. Jackie Bouvier, troubled by her parents' divorce, missed her father dearly. He remained, however, a constant force in her life, by his weekly visits, which were filled with fun and adventure, and by his frequent letters and phone calls. Selena's musical career was soaring, in no small way as a result of her father's devotion to her—by the example of his own musical talent and by his love and support. After her premature death in 1995, her father struggled with his grief and sense of emptiness.

Some fathers, busy with their careers when their children are young, devote more time later, leaving them both enriched for the effort. When Bonnie Raitt was growing up, her dad was often on the road. She struggled through her teens, while finding a musical career as her dad had. Now, as adults, the two share their different music styles with each other in performances, communicating much more than music in the process.

Some fathers demonstrate devotion by committing themselves to a career, hobby, or major interest. These fathers communicate excitement; their children watch and learn, while often developing a similar fascination. Young Alexander Graham Bell watched his father and his grandfather study the function of sound. The two men labored to understand speech and to cure speech impediments. Later, Alexander, fascinated with the vocal organs, studied how speech could be produced mechanically. By 1877, he had invented the telephone. Luciano Pavarotti spent his childhood hearing his father singing after he'd come home from his job as a bread maker. Pearl S. Buck, raised by a father who toiled endlessly as a missionary to bring God to the Chinese people, later spun tales about these same people in her fiction. Johann Christian Bach watched his father, Johann Sebastian Bach, dedicate his entire life to music. His son carried on his musical legacy.

Whether by their devotion to their children or by their devotion to a major interest or career, these fathers indelibly influenced their offspring. The following stories illustrate the timeless messages they imparted.

FAMOUS CHILD: Paul Simon

FATHER'S NAME: Louis Simon

PAPA SAID: *"That's nice, Paul—you have a nice voice."*

usic was a big part of the Simon family's life. Louis Simon was a well-respected bass player who played regularly on the Arthur Godfrey and Jackie Gleason television shows. He encouraged musicianship in his son and bought him an acoustic guitar at age fourteen. But as supportive as Louis was of his son's musical gifts, a neighborhood friend would have an even greater impact.

Paul and his nine-year-old Long Island school classmate Arthur Garfunkel sang together in a musical production of *Alice and Wonderland* in third grade. The words of praise from his dad—a professional musician—encouraged Paul as he practiced for the play in the family bathroom. The play was a hit, and soon Paul and Arthur were singing at school concerts and dances. First known as *Tom and Jerry* and influenced by the music of the Everly Brothers, the pair signed their first record contract at fifteen. Their first hit, "Hey Schoolgirl," got them on Dick Clark's *American Bandstand* TV show in 1957, but it took a few more years before they found success as the soon-to-be-world-famous duo of Simon and Garfunkel. In one of the songs on their 1970 hit album *Bridge Over Troubled Water*, entitled "Baby Driver," Paul referred to a "family bassman." In his typically modest fashion, Paul Simon officially recognized in lyrics his bassman dad, who bought him his first guitar years before.

SOURCES:

Paul Simon, Still Crazy After All These Years, Patrick Humphries (Doubleday, New York, 1989).

Simon and Garfunkel, Robert Matthew-Walker (Hippocrene Books, New York, 1984).

FAMOUS CHILD: Jacqueline Bouvier Kennedy Onassis

FATHER'S NAME: John Vernou Bouvier III

PAPA SAID: *"I suppose it won't be long until I lose you to some funny-looking gink who you think is wonderful because he is so romantic-looking in the evening and wears his mother's pearl earrings for dress-shirt buttons, because he loves her so. . . . However, perhaps you'll use your head and wait until you are at least twenty-one."*

Jacqueline Lee Bouvier was her father's first child. John Vernou Bouvier III, a thirty-eight-year-old stockbroker, had been "one of New York's most eligible bachelors." Frequently referred to as Black Jack or the Black Prince, the fun-loving and charming Jack Bouvier attracted attention wherever he went.

Jacqueline Bouvier, a strong competitor and tomboy, loved horses and her dad, not necessarily in that order. Her parents' separation when she was seven, and their subsequent divorce when she was eleven, devastated her. But Jack Bouvier continued to see Jackie and her sister, Lee, often—making a commitment to his daughters that would last his lifetime.

Jackie and Lee looked forward to these visits all week, never knowing just where Jack would take them, but knowing that the trips would be filled with fun and adventure. Their favorite places were the Bronx Zoo; Belmont Park, for the horse races; Central Park; the Metropolitan Museum of Art; Schrafft's, for lunch; Baker's Field, to watch the baseball tryouts in the spring and football in the fall; and Fifth Avenue, to shop. A favorite pastime was to put down a deposit, "borrow" the saddest and most forlorn dogs from pet shops, and play with them in Central Park all afternoon.

Before long, Jackie enrolled at boarding school, where she kept a picture of her dad in her room. Her father was a frequent weekend visitor, participating in father-daughter tennis matches and attending plays and horse shows. He also subscribed to the school paper, *Salmagundy*, where she was on staff.

At Vassar, Jackie began to date more regularly. Her frequent weekend visits to Princeton and Yale, instead of to New York City to visit her father, elicited a stern rebuke: "A woman can have wealth and beauty and brains, but without a reputation she has nothing."

Throughout his life, Jack Bouvier had difficulty managing money, struggled with alcohol addiction and career focus, and fought a battle with depression. When he was, however, with his daughters, the world was bright, the future held all promise, and the day brought great adventure.

SOURCE:
A Woman Named Jackie, C. David Heymann (Signet, New York, 1989).

FAMOUS CHILD:	Bonnie Lynn Raitt
FATHER'S NAME:	John Raitt

PAPA... *sang the lyrics from the "Soliloquy" from the Broadway show* Carousel *to his daughter, Bonnie Raitt, on the stage of the Boston Pops.*

"**B**onnie Raitt," according to author Mark Bego, "was born into a house of music" in Burbank, California, the middle child and only girl in a family of three children. Bonnie's father, John Raitt, a singer on both stage and screen, met Bonnie's mother while doing a college alumni production of *The Vagabond King*. After receiving a guitar as a Christmas gift at the age of eight, Bonnie worked hard to emulate her favorite performers. With a love of music as strong as her father's, Bonnie's career had begun.

Bonnie and her brothers spent most summers at camp in the

Adirondacks while their father toured the country performing. As Bonnie grew into her teens, she rebelled against her family's "strict, old-time values" and missed her father, who continued to spend most of his time on the road. At the same time, the family's Quaker religion, with its strong belief in pacifism, thrust her into the war protest movement in the 1960s. Music offered her comfort.

As a student at Radcliffe, Bonnie attended Cambridge blues and jazz clubs. Soon, she began opening for the musicians and performing on college campuses, and started finding the academic life less and less important. Leaving Radcliffe behind, she became a full-time blues singer.

Years later, in televised performance of the Boston Pops, as John Raitt sang the "Soliloquy" from *Carousel*—a sentimental song sung by a father about his pending fatherhood—Bonnie emerged from the wings to complete the song with him.

Having survived the difficulties experienced by many parents and teens, John Raitt and his daughter shared a new relationship—one of mutual respect and devotion. Bonnie stated, "I anticipated it being incredibly moving, and it was." John Raitt, after having spent most of his music career on the road, now has more time to connect with his daughter. While sharing their different music styles, they have found a common connection—perhaps "just in the nick of time."

DEVOTION

SOURCE:
Bonnie Raitt—Just in the Nick of Time, Mark Bego (Birch Lane Press, New York, 1995).

FAMOUS CHILD: Luciano Pavarotti

FATHER'S NAME: Fernando Pavarotti

PAPA SAID: *"The moment is ripe, now or never. My legs turned to butter. I broke out in a cold sweat, but I managed to make it to the stage."*

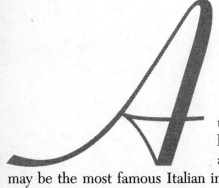

uthor Candido Bonvicini opens his biography of Luciano Pavarotti with these words: "He may be the most famous Italian in the world, but in Modena he is still 'the tenor's son.'" Luciano's father, Fernando, a lyric tenor, supported his family by baking bread in his shop and singing at weddings and community events. With a devotion to his family and his music, he filled the apartment with recordings of the great singers. Fernando describes his "genuine passion for his job" and the fact that he "never had the courage to take risks" as reasons why he never pursued a career in opera himself.

Surrounded by women—mother, aunts, a younger sister—

Luciano and his family lived in public housing, where sixteen units of the building were filled with friends and relatives. Adele Pavarotti remembers her son climbing on a stool at the age of three and proclaiming, "My daddy is a tenor, and I am a little tenor." Luciano himself remembers that one of his first stages was the courtyard of his apartment, where he exercised his vocal talents to the approval of his neighbors—as long as "he didn't decide to perform too early in the morning or late at night," according to Bonvicini.

At eight, Luciano and his family reluctantly left Modena for a farm outside of town, fleeing the danger of war. Luciano remembers singing in the fields as the family struggled at the height of the war. Because of the importance of his profession to the war effort, Fernando was able to avoid the fighting but ran into trouble with a militant officer who placed him in jail. When the order was subsequently given to select those for relocation to a concentration camp, a second officer remembered Fernando's talents at making good bread and he was sent home to his relieved family.

As a teenager, Luciano began to think about a career as a math or science teacher or physical education instructor, but decided that his attending college would cause too much of a financial burden on his family. Instead he made the decision to continue his voice studies and to support himself by selling insurance part-time. Inspired by one of Modena's great tenors—

his father—Luciano had decided to entertain the world with his songs.

In 1980, on the stage of a New York theater, Luciano Pavarotti performed to an audience of six thousand people as his father proudly watched from a first-row seat. Suddenly Luciano announced, "Now you will hear my father." With his "legs turned to butter," Fernando Pavarotti walked to the stage. In front of a supportive audience, he sang the words of César Franck's *Panis Angelicus* with his lyrical tenor voice. Years of fear melted away. The floodlights blocked his view of the thousands of people before him as he sang as he had never sung before. At the conclusion of the performance, Luciano hugged his dad while exclaiming, "Bravo, Pavarotti," as father and son basked in the hearty applause.

SOURCE:
The Tenor's Son—My Days with Pavarotti, Candido Bonvicini (St. Martin's Press, New York, 1989).

FAMOUS CHILD:	Nichelle Nichols
FATHER'S NAME:	Samuel Earl Nichols Sr.

PAPA SAID: *"If she works hard, in two, three years, she will be ready for any corps de ballet in the world."*

*F*or Nichelle Nichols, known to "Trekkies" as Lieutenant Uhura, the communications officer of *Star Trek*'s U.S.S. *Enterprise*, her father was her hero. In the early thirties he was the mayor of Robbins, Illinois, a small town southwest of Chicago and one of only four American towns then governed by a black. But he was a lot more to his daughter. Nichelle notes, "He instilled in each of us that we were special." Once, while showing her a book of snowflake illustrations, he pointed out, "Each is different, yet each is uniquely perfect." She recalls, "In our house, it was understood that whatever occupation you chose was not important: *You* were."

With a total devotion to his daughter's development as a performing artist, Sam closely monitored her career every step of the way. At the age of fourteen, Nichelle had an appointment to audition at the Chicago Ballet Academy. When the ballet master found out that Nichelle was black, he said, "Black people cannot dance the ballet." Sam immediately and firmly replied, "We have an appointment for you to see her dance. We are here." Nichelle performed beautifully and was subsequently accepted. Her ballet experience quickly translated into a wide variety of dance opportunities—including one several years later with the legend Duke Ellington.

Nichelle was strengthened by her father's early devotion, and applied it to her blossoming career. In her *Star Trek* role, Nichelle became the first African-American woman to have a major continuing role on television. Whoopi Goldberg noted the significance of this, stating that when she was a kid growing up in the projects, Lieutenant Uhura was "the only vision of black people in the future."

In a eulogy to *Star Trek* founder Gene Roddenberry, Nichelle noted, "Like all of Gene's characters, Uhura embodied humankind's highest values and lived according to principles that he was certain would one day guide all human endeavor." While her testimony was directed toward the creator of her fictional character, the ideals she expressed were not

---

DEVOTION

inconsistent with those she'd learned from her father years
ago.

SOURCE:
Beyond Uhura, Star Trek and Other Memories, Nichelle Nichols (G. P. Putnam's Sons, New York, 1994).

FAMOUS CHILD: Arthur Fiedler

FATHER'S NAME: Emanuel Fiedler

PAPA SAID: *"You don't want to go to college, and now you've decided business doesn't appeal to you. There seems to be only one thing left for you to do. Would you like to try music?"*

*T*his advice from Emanuel Fiedler to his son, the future Boston Pops conductor, came in the summer of 1911. The family lived in Berlin, where Austrian-born Emanuel was a symphony concertmaster and music teacher. Emanuel, a graduate of the Vienna Conservatory, had been a violinist with the Boston Symphony shortly after its founding in 1881, just before Arthur's birth. Arthur Fiedler's first birthday in 1885 marked the start of the Symphony's "Promenade Concerts"—a forerunner to the Boston Pops.

Arthur grew up in Boston, in the shadow of Symphony Hall. Explaining that "music was the only religion in our family," Arthur noted that his parents were firm, insisting on regular practice for Arthur and his sisters, Rosa and Elsa, who also developed music careers. Emanuel's first question on arriving home each evening would be, "Did you practice today?"

With a fervent childhood desire to be either a streetcar conductor or fireman, Arthur eventually, like his father, devoted his life to the field of music, saying, "I was not pushed into it." When Emanuel's career took the family to Berlin, Arthur enrolled in the Royal Academy of Music, crediting his father's tutoring for his having been one of only thirteen applicants accepted by the Academy. By nineteen, Arthur had progressed to the point where he was offered a position at a German opera house. World War I intervened, however, and fearing that he would be drafted into the German Army, he returned to Boston to join the Boston Symphony in 1915.

Arthur Fiedler began a fifty-year tenure as the conductor of the Boston Pops in 1929, serving until his death in 1979. Demonstrating his lifelong interest in firefighting, Arthur Fiedler occasionally donned a fire chief's hat during his concerts, to the delight of his audience.

SOURCE:
Fiedler, the Colorful Mr. Pops—The Man and His Music, Robin Moore (Little, Brown, Boston, 1968).

FAMOUS CHILD: Alexander Graham Bell

FATHER'S NAME: Alexander Melville Bell

PAPA SAID: *"You have fairly won the honor by rendering yourself one of the foremost men in the United States."*

*E*dinburgh, Scotland, often called "the Athens of the North" because of its long association with leading writers, philosophers, and scientists, continued its influence with the birth of Alexander Graham Bell. The third Alexander in three consecutive generations of Bells, Alexander Graham Bell's lifework, according to author Robert V. Bruce, "much more than usual grew out of what his father and grandfather had done before him."

Alexander Melville Bell had worked with his own father, Alexander Bell, in the field of speech, public speaking, and the treatment of speech impediments, leading him to the lifelong study of vocal organs. He taught at the University of Edinburgh, traveled to Canada and the United States, and became even more deeply involved in the field of the deaf when he married Eliza Symonds, who was partially deaf. Throughout his childhood, Alexander Graham Bell translated church sermons for his mother by pronouncing the words distinctly directly next to her face.

In 1863, Alexander Melville and his teenage sons traveled to London to call on Sir Charles Wheatstone, one of England's leading scientists, who had worked with electricity as well as with the science of sound. They were eager to see Sir Wheatstone's version of an eighteenth-century mechanical imitation of the human voice. After returning home, Alexander challenged his sons, Alexander Graham and Melly, to make a version of their own. Using cotton, rubber bands, wood, tubes, a tin horn, and a lamb's larynx that they'd gotten from a local butcher, the boys replicated a human head, with tongue, nasal passages, lips, cheeks, and throat which, when manipulated, made humanlike sounds. Alexander Melville Bell was impressed. His sons had not only learned how the organs of speech worked, but also how speech was produced.

Alexander Graham Bell taught at schools for deaf children in Scotland and the United States; although, in the tradition of three generations of Bells, he was always devoted to his studies and to research, Bruce wrote that "to the day of his death, he would proudly count himself above all else a teacher of the deaf." His marriage to Mabel Hubbard in 1877 brought him even closer to the world of the deaf, for Mabel, like his mother, was deaf herself.

On February 12, 1877 at Lyceum Hall in Salem, Massachusetts, a full house of ticket-holders gathered to hear thirty-year-old Alexander Graham Bell lecture at the Essex Institute. As Thomas A. Watson spoke eighteen miles away in Exeter Place in Boston, his voice was transmitted to the eager, standing-room-only crowd in Salem. The entire audience strained to listen as Watson's voice came out of the small box on the stage. The sound of his songs and news reports were heard throughout the hall. A *Boston Globe* reporter called the demonstration "an unqualified success" and in a headline run the next day said:

SENT BY TELEPHONE
THE FIRST NEWSPAPER DISPATCH SENT
BY A HUMAN VOICE OVER THE WIRES

The first telephone was born.

Years later, and by now a resident of the United States, Alexander Graham Bell was elected to the American Academy of Arts and Sciences. His father proudly responded, "You have fairly won the honor by rendering yourself one of the foremost men in the United States."

SOURCE:
Alexander Graham Bell—And the Conquest of Solitude, Robert V. Bruce, (Little, Brown, Boston, 1973).

FAMOUS CHILD:	Cal Ripken Jr.
FATHER'S NAME:	Cal Ripken Sr. (Rip)

PAPA SAID: *"The Orioles have always provided a home for the Ripkens."*

*T*he father of the man who set a record for most consecutive major league baseball games played (all with the Orioles) first became a part of the Baltimore Orioles organization in 1956 as a minor-league player, and continued with them as a player, scout, coach, and manager until the 1980s. This took him away from his family frequently. In fact, he was in the Orioles minor-league team in Fox Cities, Wisconsin, in 1960 when his first son, Cal Junior, was born. Cal Senior batted in the winning run that day.

The Ripken children grew up around baseball. They traveled with their father. They moved as his career took him to different cities, and when he was home, they were at the ballpark watching him play. Cal Junior states that baseball was never forced on him, and his mom, Vi, adds, "Ever since Cal was old enough to walk, Cal always wanted to be a ballplayer."

He idolized his father. When Cal Junior was nine, he went to clinics conducted by his father and to his games. He says, "I came early to the ballpark and shagged in the outfield because I knew he'd be proud of me for doing that. And it seemed like Dad's job was the best job you could have in the world."

Rip's schedule took him away from home frequently, and Cal Junior recalls that when he was home, life focused on baseball—from watching games to discussing the day's events on the field and hearing his dad's bedtime stories about the old days of the game.

He also benefited from advice given to him by many of the Orioles players. His skills developed, and after a notable high school career he was drafted by the Orioles in 1978. After a few minor-league seasons, he was brought up to the majors by Baltimore. In 1982, he started a streak of consecutive games that by 1995 had extended past the 2,130 games played by the legendary Lou Gehrig. For several seasons, Cal Senior managed and brother Bill played alongside.

SOURCE:
Ironman, The Cal Ripken, Jr. Story, Harvey Rosenfeld (St. Martin's Press, New York, 1995).

FAMOUS CHILD:	Pearl S. Buck
FATHER'S NAME:	Andrew Sydenstricker

PAPA ASKED: *"How much will you make from this book?"*

She answered, "Twenty thousand dollars." (She eventually made more than $1 million.)

He responded, "That's very nice, I'm sure, but I'm afraid I can't undertake it."

Described as a "fisher of men" by his daughter, Andrew Sydenstricker distinguished himself as a missionary, a Chinese scholar, a translator of the New Testament from Greek to Chinese, and a lover of ancient languages. He devoted his entire life to spreading the word of God throughout rural China. After Pearl wrote her 1932 Pulitzer Prize–winning book, *The Good Earth*, a novel about the people of China, she showed it to her father. The intense, practical, and religious man just didn't understand fiction.

Although born in Hillsboro, West Virginia, while her parents were home on leave, Pearl spent her childhood in a small home along the Yangtze River, tended by her mother as well as by a Chinese nurse and learning Chinese as her first language. She enjoyed hours of stories told by her Chinese nurse and read many books, inspiring her to write at a young age.

With a missionary zeal similar to her father's and an intense love for the Chinese people, Pearl Buck dedicated her life to writing down their stories and culture in her works of fiction. She also worked tirelessly for humanitarian causes on behalf of orphaned Asian and retarded children.

After her father's death in 1932, Pearl Buck went to visit his grave on top of a hill in China. She wrote, "I stayed for hours, remembering his long and brilliant life, so little appreciated or even understood by his fellow missionaries. There was something symbolic in this lofty resting place, the noble mountains encircling, and the wind blowing the clouds down from the sky."

By 1936, Pearl Buck's highly acclaimed biography of her father's life, *Fighting Angel—Portrait of a Soul*, was in the bookstores and doing well. In 1938, she received a Nobel Prize for Literature.

SOURCE:
Pearl S. Buck—A Biography, Theodore F. Harris (John Day, New York, 1969).

FAMOUS CHILD:	Johann Christian Bach
FATHER'S NAME:	Johann Sebastian Bach

PAPA SAID: *"I can arrange a fine concert with voices and instruments, using only members of my family."*

*J*ohann Sebastian Bach lived his life for music. He was a composer and the cantor of St. Thomas Church in Leipzig, Germany, so music filled his days. And it gave him no small sense of pride to know that two of his first wife's children were gifted and devoted to music as well.

By the age of fifty, he had married his second wife, Anna Magdalena, who presented him with his eighteenth child in 1735, Johann Christian Bach. Although his first family had presented him with two musical sons, it was this eighteenth child who would eventually attain a fame almost as great as his own. He doted on his talented son, taught him everything he knew, and rejoiced in

Johann Christian's devotion to the discipline he loved so much.

After his father's death, fifteen-year-old Johann Christian learned that his father had willed him three of his favorite instruments. Shortly thereafter, he left Leipzig, taking with him not only the instruments but also, according to author Heinz Gartner, "a solid technical foundation and a musical heritage no other young musician of his day could call his own."

After studying in Berlin, Johann Christian Bach went to England, where he was master of music to King George III in a life—much as his father's—devoted to music. Focusing on sonatas, concertos, and symphonies, and not on sacred music like his father, he influenced the music of Haydn and of Mozart, who was his greatest fan. His father would have been proud.

SOURCE:
John Christian Bach, Heinz Gärtner (Amadeus Press, Portland, translation copyright obtained in 1994).

FAMOUS CHILD:	Selena (Selena Quintanilla Perez)
FATHER'S NAME:	Abraham Quintanilla

PAPA... *established a foundation in his deceased daughter's name whose purpose is to encourage children "to complete their education, to respect human life, and to sing whatever song they were born to sing."*

Selena, in the few short years of her singing career, put the style of Tejano music on the charts and broadened its appeal from a regional one to one that was accepted internationally. Her life was tragically ended by a bullet on March 31, 1995. No one then or now felt the pain of her loss more than her devoted father, Abraham Quintanilla.

His passion was music. The passion began when he was a child and formed his own musical group, Los Dinos. Years later, when his five-year-old daughter, Selena, wanted to sing along with her older brother as he played the guitar, Abraham Quintanilla quickly recognized her talent. He would go on to form a group for his daughter, named Los Dinos in honor of his childhood band, this time with his teenage daughter, Selena, singing the lead as he had in his own band years before. The group's popularity took off.

In 1986, fifteen-year-old Selena was named the Female Vocalist and Performer of the Year at the San Antonio Tejano Music Awards. Driven largely by her phenomenal popularity, sales of Tejano records increased from two million copies in the early 1980s to over twenty-four million a decade later.

Abe was at the center of his daughter's career. He managed the band, handled the bookings, ran the sound boards, and in the early years, even drove the bus. Other spin-off enterprises were formed to capitalize on the group's success. Along with the fame came a more sultry style for the still down-to-earth Selena. While her father despised some of her costumes, author Clint Richmond in his book about Selena notes that "to Selena, they were just that, costumes." Then, in the midst of all this excitement and fame, a bullet from the gun of Selena's fan club manager ended it all.

In a newspaper interview a year after her death, Abe noted that he still cries for Selena every day. Now a Jehovah's Witness, Abe finds hope in a belief that he will one day be reunited with his daughter.

DEVOTION

SOURCES:
Selena! The Phenomenal Life and Tragic Death of the Tejano Music Queen, Clint Richmond (Pocket Books, New York, 1995).

Articles by Ron George, staff writer for *Corpus Christi Caller-Times* on the Selena website: http://www.caller.com/selena/

Famous Child:	Woodrow Wilson (Thomas Wilson)
Father's Name:	Reverend Joseph Ruggles Wilson
Papa Said:	*"My precious son."*

The relationship between the future President of the United States and his Presbyterian minister father was one of utmost devotion. Ray S. Baker, official Wilson biographer, points out, "Letters between the two can be called nothing but love letters." The salutations usually read, "My beloved father," "My precious son," or "Darling boy."

Their closeness started early as the somewhat sickly child was often embraced and hugged by his protective father. The Reverend Wilson guided his son's early education through the Scriptures with the intent that his son would someday also be a Presbyterian minister. And young Tommy, always impressed with his father's orations from the pulpit, did excel in any subject that involved speaking. His father's devotion convinced him that he was destined for greatness. It's also claimed that for the first forty years of his life, Wilson never made a major decision without consulting his father.

When he enrolled at Princeton University in 1875, the future President discovered politics and was intrigued by the British government and the orations of the nineteenth-century prime minister William Gladstone, who physically resembled his handsome father. He later used these same skills as the president of Princeton University and the governor of New Jersey. In 1912, Woodrow Wilson was elected President of the United States, and in this capacity led the country through World War I.

Reverend Wilson died shortly after his son became president of Princeton. Sigmund Freud and William Bullitt, in a psychological study of Wilson, suggested that his father's death stimulated Woodrow Wilson's addiction to speech-making. They wrote, "His concept of statesmanship always remained the picture of a minister laying down the law of God to his flock. Ultimately the White House became his pulpit and the world his congregation."

Adding that Wilson "never grew beyond his fatherly identification," and that the two men possessed similar defects and strengths, Bullitt and Freud claim that just as his father was unable to translate the messages of his sermons into reality, President Wilson was unable to translate all of the Fourteen Points he had espoused as terms for ending World War I into reality in the Treaty of Versailles.

SOURCE:
Woodrow Wilson, a Psychological Study, Sigmund Freud and William Bullitt (Houghton Mifflin, Boston, 1967).

FAMOUS CHILD:	Candice Bergen
FATHER'S NAME:	Edgar Bergen

PAPA SAID: *"Now, now, please, Charlie. Candy, my own little Candy, tonight is the happiest night of my life. Tonight, my little girl steps out into the footlights of life. . . ."*

Edgar Bergen was at the top of his career. He had a television show. He had a "dummy" named Charlie McCarthy. America was fascinated. And now his only child was on his show for the first time. With Charlie on his knee, Edgar Bergen introduced his precocious six-year-old daughter to the audience at home. Candice Bergen had made her television debut.

As the celebrity child of Edgar Bergen, Candice Bergen grew up among the "rich and famous." "Uncle Walt" Disney, John Barrymore, Katharine Hepburn, Ira Gershwin, Ronald Reagan, and James Stewart were all visitors to the Bergen home. Weekends were special times for Candice as her father, a pilot, took her on short trips by plane. The greatest competition for her father's time and attention, however, would come from her only "sibling," the wooden dummy named Charlie McCarthy.

Edgar Bergen started out with a profound love of vaudeville. Raised on a farm, he would often sneak under the local vaudeville tent to watch the entertainment inside. These shows traveled throughout America's towns and cities before the advent of television and attracted scores of fans. At the age of eleven, Edgar paid a quarter for a book called *The Wizard's Manual*, from which he learned magic tricks and ventriloquism, eventually "throwing his voice into his mother's apple pies and creating a house alive with voices," according to Candice.

By the age of sixteen, Edgar had succeeded in creating a character who resembled an outgoing and witty newspaper boy in the neighborhood. Commissioning a friend, Mr. Mack, to carve a dummy out of wood, Edgar named him "Charlie" after the newspaper boy and "McCarthy" in honor of the wood-carver. Although a college student at Northwestern, he continued to perform with Charlie, and subsequently dropped out of college as he and Charlie McCarthy became more and more successful on the vaudeville circuit.

Dignitaries and performers from throughout the world gathered for Edgar Bergen's funeral, among them Jim Henson, who had dedicated his first Muppet movie "to the magic of Edgar Bergen." Candice Bergen, with a long television and movie career

DEVOTION

to her name and having benefited greatly from the lifelong devotion of her father, related that the funeral "paid honor and humor to a man who gave amply to the world of both. It was the farewell he deserved."

FAMOUS CHILD: Pablo Picasso (Pablo Ruiz)

FATHER'S NAME: Don José Ruiz y Blasco

PAPA SAID: *"In hands you see the hand."*

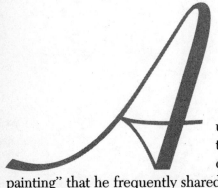

uthor Patrick O'Brian refers to this "gnomic utterance" as one of Don José's "dictums on painting" that he frequently shared with his son, Pablo Ruiz, later known as Picasso. That isn't all he shared.

Don José Ruiz y Blasco, a museum curator, created realistic, representational paintings using his excellent knowledge of artistic technique. Young Pablo watched and learned as his own skills quickly surpassed those of his father.

With a household full of women (mother, grandmother, aunts, and female cousins), his time with his father was special. Don José posed for Pablo's well-known work *First Communion*—done when the boy was just fourteen—and provided his young son his own studio a year later. Later, after again posing for his son, in the painting *Science and Charity*, Don José was thrilled when it won honorable mention in the prestigious Madrid Fine Arts Exhibition, and scraped enough money together to send Pablo to Paris to study. Finally, Don José, despairing of ever becoming a great artist himself and certain he had taught Pablo everything he knew, handed over his own brushes to his son. He never painted again.

O'Brian describes this father-and-son relationship as "immensely complex." Pablo occasionally "split" from his father for periods of time, but continued to use his father as a model throughout his career. He took his maternal family surname, Picasso, which was highly unusual for the time, but always spoke of his father with "great affection and respect," according to the author.

In the 1930s, well after he had attained worldwide fame, Picasso spoke of his father. "Every time I draw a man, automatically I think of my father. As far as I am concerned *the man* is Don José, and that will be as long as I live."

SOURCES:

Picasso—A Biography, Patrick O'Brian (G. P. Putnam's Sons, New York, 1976).

Picasso—Portrait of Picasso as a Young Man, Norman Mailer (Atlantic Monthly Press, New York, 1995).

FAMOUS CHILD:	Madame Curie (Marie "Manya" Salomée Sklodowski)
FATHER'S NAME:	Vladislav Sklodowski

PAPA... *"wisely decided that Manya needed a prolonged rest, and he shipped her off to the country for a year."*

—Author Rosalynd Pflaum

*I*t was a difficult sixteen years. Professor Vladislav Sklodowski taught at a school for boys, where he was given housing for his wife and five children. When Marie was five, her mother developed tuberculosis, and she never fully regained her health. Eventually Vladislav lost his job—let go by the school's director, who was distinctly anti-Polish in a country that favored Russian culture and politics. Money was tight, so the family moved to a small apartment and took in boarders to meet expenses, often boarding up to ten people, requiring that Marie sleep on a couch in the dining room. During this time, Marie's elder sister died of tuberculosis, and two years later her mother did too. Vladislav never fully recovered financially, personally, or professionally from these tragic events, but remained always proud and supportive of his bright young daughter.

Every Saturday night throughout Marie's childhood, Vladislav read to the children from the classics, devoted as he was to their education. By the time her father's career faded and boarders came to live with the family, Marie had developed such an intense ability to concentrate in the small, noisy, busy apartment that her studies hardly suffered. The same girl who had started reading at the age of four graduated at sixteen with top honors in a system that made it difficult to achieve if you were Polish. But there was a price: She was sick and exhausted. Her father decided that she needed a year of rest in the country with no schoolbooks, no studies, and no schedule. At key points in her life, at times of difficulty, he was always there.

Recharged upon her return, Marie knew she must help with the family finances. Obtaining a job as a live-in tutor and governess, she sent money home to help her sister go to medical school, while improving her own math skills through correspondence with her father. She later returned to study chemistry and do experiments in the Museum of Industry and Agriculture, which had been founded by a cousin of hers. (The "museum" was actually a front for a college; there were no laws against teaching Polish students in a museum.)

Before long, Marie had saved enough to go to the Sorbonne

in Paris, from which she graduated first in her class. After returning home, she again was exhausted. Vladislav, proud of his daughter's academic success, catered to her all summer until she felt well once again.

After her marriage to Pierre, Marie Curie, now Madame Curie, continued her work. With her husband, she discovered polonium and radium, while exploring the use of radiation. During her first pregnancy, as she struggled with morning sickness, she turned again to her father, who took her on a vacation to a small fishing village in Brittany.

At his death in 1902, Marie was inconsolable. Her earliest supporter in her intense quest for knowledge was gone—but not, at least, until he had witnessed her success as a scientist.

SOURCE:
Grand Obsession—Madame Curie and Her World, Rosalynd Pflaum (Doubleday, New York, 1989).

FAMOUS CHILD:	Eleanor Roosevelt
	(Anna Eleanor Roosevelt)
FATHER'S NAME:	Elliott Roosevelt

PAPA WROTE: *"The next time you are walking, go by a house that is being built. Watch the workmen bring one stone after another and place it on the one gone before. Then think there are a lot of funny little workmen running about in your small golden head called 'Ideas,' which are carrying a lot of stones like 'Facts.' These 'Ideas' are being directed by your teachers in various ways. These 'Fact Stones' are alongside each other in your dear Golden Head until they build a beautiful house called 'Education.'"*

Anna Eleanor Roosevelt knew she was important—knew she had someone in her corner. Born into a world of wealth, but awkward and plain as a child, she treasured her father's attention. Called "a miracle from heaven" at birth and "Little Nell" as a youngster, Eleanor was soothed by her father's words. And then he was gone. His words of advice, however, were never forgotten.

To Elliott Roosevelt, life was a perpetual struggle—not for wealth or social standing, but for sobriety. In the middle of this struggle, however, there was his Little Nell, and all the hope that his bright young daughter symbolized. She listened to his poetry and was his constant companion. He brought her on his visits to the New York Orthopedic Hospital, founded by his father, where he volunteered on behalf of crippled children.

While away from home fighting his losing battle with alcohol, Elliott regularly wrote his daughter words of devotion and encouragement. In 1892, Eleanor's mother died of diphtheria, and two years later her father, never having conquered his disease and leaving his ten-year-old daughter with some wonderful memories and these words of advice.

After husband Franklin Delano Roosevelt's inauguration as President, Eleanor became a tireless and devoted worker for social causes—especially the civil rights of blacks and women—hosted her own radio program, and wrote a syndicated newspaper column. Eventually she was appointed United States delegate to the United Nations and helped draft the United Nations Declaration of Human Rights. In 1951, while referring to her father, Eleanor Roosevelt said, "He lives in my dreams to this day."

SOURCE:
Eleanor Roosevelt, Richard Harrity and Ralph G. Martin (Duell, Sloan and Pearce, New York, 1958).

FAMOUS CHILD:	Liza Minnelli
FATHER'S NAME:	Vincente Minnelli
PAPA SAID:	*"Everybody searches for a little magic."*

*L*iza Minnelli is in a unique position as the celebrity child of two celebrities. She was born less than a year after singer/actress Judy Garland married director Vincente Minnelli, whom she had met while working on the 1944 hit movie *Meet Me in St. Louis*. Liza made her acting debut at the age of three in the last scene of her mother's *In the Good Old Summertime*.

Though her parents' marriage broke apart when Liza was just seven, she continued to receive from both their loving attention. Vincente often took his daughter to work with him, where she proudly proclaimed, "I'm just the director's daughter." He arranged to have her photographed in special custom-made costumes. Liza credits some of the stars she met as a child with influencing her own career later. She describes Fred Astaire's dance routine in the Minnelli-directed movie *The Band Wagon* as a perfect example of her father's belief that "everybody searches for a little magic."

Vincente Minnelli admitted in his autobiography that he smothered his daughter with love, but explained, "If I spoiled Liza outrageously, the fairy tale quality of our relationship achieved a balance with the starkness of her life with Judy." Liza admits, "I was always Daddy's girl. He was so wonderful, supportive, patient."

Vincente Minnelli died while Liza was touring with Frank Sinatra in 1986. Ironically, Sinatra, the first visitor to see Liza when she was born, was the one who told her of her father's death. Four years later, Liza organized an eight-week retrospective tribute to her father, which opened on Father's Day at the Los Angeles County Museum of Art. After the show was over, she walked outside, looked up to the sky, and wished her father a happy Father's Day.

SOURCE:
Liza, Born a Star, Wendy Leigh (Penguin, New York, 1993).

FAITH

Nat King Cole
Menachem Begin
Emily Dickinson
Oral Roberts
Susan B. Anthony
Ansel Adams

FAITH

*F*aith is rooted in a personal belief that is often affiliated with religion, but not always. Whether a father has passed on a religious affiliation, an ideal, or a love of nature, he has given his child a safety net upon which to cling during times of challenge.

The Reverend Coles knew where his strength came from—it came from his God. In a nightclub in Chicago, Nat King Cole sang "Straighten Up and Fly Right"—a song based on words from one of his father's sermons. Years later, Nat's daughter performed the same song. And Natalie Cole states, "There's always a flavor of gospel in what I do."

Faith can be represented by political belief. Menachem Begin always remembered how his father talked of a future land—a "Land of Israel." In a political career that championed the eventual formation of this country, Menachem Begin achieved his goal, and that of his father as well. In 1977, Prime Minister Menachem Begin welcomed Egypt's president, Anwar Sadat, to his country with the words, "We have one wish—we want to bring peace to our people."

Emily Dickinson grew up in a family held together by a strong belief in God. She wasn't, however, ever able to worship or believe in just the same way as they. This religious struggle dominated her adult life, and eventually translated into her lifelong love of nature. Through her poems, Emily Dickinson continues to communicate this love to her generations of readers.

Whether as a religious or political belief or a love of the natural world, faith is a comfort in times of difficulty. American poet John Greenleaf Whittier wrote, "The steps of faith fall on the seeming void, but find the rock beneath." The child who receives this rock, or safety net, receives a priceless gift.

FAMOUS CHILD:	**Nat King Cole** **(Nathaniel Adams Coles)**
FATHER'S NAME:	**Reverend Edward James Coles Jr.**
PAPA SAID:	*"Tone it down, son, or take the consequences."*

*N*at King Cole's parents moved to the South Side of Chicago from Montgomery, Alabama, hoping for more freedom and opportunity than the South in the early 1900s could provide. The close-knit family centered its activities on the church, where Nat's father, the Reverend Edward James Coles Jr., was a pastor and his mother, Perlina, played the organ and led the choir. The Reverend Coles, a strong moral leader, loved his God and his family and expected his children's respect and obedience, accompanied by good behavior and a strong work ethic.

Perlina insisted that the children learn the piano and have a love for music, and that they did. Reverend Coles, fond of more conservative church music, never approved of his son's forays into popular music. Occasionally Nat, while playing the organ during church services, just couldn't help embellishing gospel melodies with flourishes of jazz, prompting his father's stern rebuke. The conflict between father and son was finally resolved with Perlina Coles' assistance. If Nat would play the organ obediently in church for his father, he could play jazz piano in the clubs on weeknights.

By the age of sixteen, Nat had formed a big band of ten to fourteen pieces in the tradition of Duke Ellington and began writing arrangements and songs—one of them based on a lesson his father had taught him at home. Echoing one of his dad's pleas with his South Side congregation to "straighten up and fly right," Nat King Cole wrote a song of the same name urging his listeners to follow Christian beliefs and do the right thing, no matter how difficult it might be.

As proud as Reverend Coles was of his son's considerable musical ability, he could never understand why none of his sons wanted to become a preacher. Years later, in his north Chicago church during a visit by his famous son, Nat King Cole, and while surrounded by hordes of his son's young fans, Reverend Coles preached, "Nat can send you with his songs. You come to church, I'll send you with my sermons." According to Perlina, though Nat had graduated from gospel hymns to jazz, he never forgot to do his church work.

In 1990, Nat King Cole's daughter, Natalie Cole, ascended the stage, nominated for a Grammy Award for "Miss You Like Crazy." She burst into "Straighten Up and Fly Right" with singing legend Ella Fitzgerald, and the next generation of the Cole family's extraordinary musical talent was launched. The faith that had defined her grandfather's very existence and continued through her father's musical creativity and church work had now reached down to her life. And indeed, Natalie Cole says, "There's always a flavor of gospel in what I do. I miss it when it's not there."

SOURCE:
Unforgettable: The Life and Mystique of Nat King Cole, Leslie Gourse (St. Martin's Press, New York, 1991).

FAMOUS CHILD:	Menachem Begin
FATHER'S NAME:	Dov Zeev Begin

PAPA SAID: *"The day will come when we will all be in the Land of Israel."*

ov Zeev was a popular leader in the Jewish community of Brisk (formerly Brest Litovsk), Poland, where he met the leading Zionist leaders of the day. During World War I, Brisk changed hands twice, being run first by the Germans, then by the Polish, and finally by the Bolsheviks. After the war, Dov Zeev Begin rallied the community and rebuilt the synagogue as well as many homes, believing that a "Land of Israel" would eventually be born.

As a child, Menachem Begin listened to his father and his father's friends talk, subsequently forming a Zionist political stance similar to theirs. As a ten-year-old, he accompanied his father to a festival that he had organized. In front of an admiring audience and while standing on a table, he described the festival's significance to him and amazed the audience with his oratorical talent. The religious and political inspiration that Menachem derived from these festivals continued throughout his life, according to author Eitan Haber.

During World War I, Dov Zeev had faith that Poland would survive, and dreamed of the day when a Land of Israel would be his home. By the age of eighteen, Menachem had entered law school at Warsaw University, spent time in a Soviet prison camp during World War II, and lost his father and many other relatives in the Holocaust. Sustained by his father's vision—the Land of Israel—Menachem continued his political and religious mission.

In 1977, Menachem Begin stood before the Israeli parliament on the occasion of Egyptian president Anwar Sadat's visit to Israel. The son of the man with the vision of a Land of Israel declared, "We have one wish in our hearts, one wish in our souls—to bring peace to our people."

SOURCE:
Menachem Begin—The Legend and the Man, Eitan Haber (Delacorte Press, New York, 1978).

FAMOUS CHILD:	Emily Dickinson
FATHER'S NAME:	Edward Dickinson

PAPA... *"is too busy with his Briefs—to notice what we do—He buys me many Books—but begs me not to read them—because he fears they joggle the mind." (Emily Dickinson)*

*E*dward Dickinson "was reared on the ideals of the eighteenth century," according to author Thomas H. Johnson, beginning his education at Amherst College before transferring and then graduating from Yale. He was the treasurer of Amherst College for thirty-eight years, served in the Massachusetts legislature for three terms and in the United States Congress for one, and devoted much of his life to community, church, and college affairs. Emily felt "from her earliest childhood a respect for her father akin to awe," according to Johnson.

Emily struggled with issues of formal religion throughout her life in a family that was conservative and churchgoing. By the time she eagerly entered Mount Holyoke Female Seminary at sixteen, her whole family and most of her college friends had embraced Christianity and become "converted." Emily loved the intellectual climate at Mount Holyoke, but became increasingly frustrated by her classmates' focus on formal religion—a conflict that plagued her all her life. The intellectual climate also threatened her conservative father, who feared that these new ideas would "joggle" her mind.

After leaving college, Emily spent increasing periods of time in her beloved Main Street home, surrounded by family and visitors, while writing in her room, tending her garden, and visiting with her brother and sister-in-law next door. Once invited by a friend to visit, Emily declined with the words, "I'm growing selfish in my dear home, but I do love it so, and when some pleasant friend invites me to spend a week with her, I look at Father, Mother, Vinnie, and all my friends, and I say no-no, I can't leave them. What if they die when I am gone?"

In 1830, while addressing the Massachusetts legislature, Edward Dickinson took ill and died two hours later at his hotel. Emily Dickinson, in a letter, wrote, "I am glad there is immortality—but would have tested it myself—before intrusting him. Home is so far from Home, since my Father died."

In the years before her death in 1886, Emily spent more and more time cloistered in her room writing poetry. Many of her poems dealt with love of nature, immortality, the sea, and the seasons, revealing a faith uniquely her own. In her poem "I Never Saw a Moor," Emily writes:

> I never saw a moor,
> I never saw the sea;
> Yet know I how the heather looks,
> And what a wave must be.
>
> I never spoke with God,
> Nor visited in heaven;
> Yet certain am I of the spot
> As if the chart were given.

Although she published only seven poems in her lifetime, she carefully constructed hundreds and hundreds more, wrapping them in little packets, tying them with ribbon, and storing them in a bureau drawer. It was only after Emily's death that her sister discovered their existence and made arrangements for their publication.

Emily Dickinson, Thomas H. Johnson (Harvard University Press, Cambridge, 1955).

FAMOUS CHILD:	Oral Roberts
FATHER'S NAME:	Ellis Roberts
PAPA SAID:	*"The time has come for you to get saved."*

*T*he doctors examined seventeen-year-old Oral and delivered a unanimous verdict: He had tuberculosis in both lungs and was in the disease's final stages. There was little hope that he would recover. To preacher Ellis Roberts, who had seen several family members die from tuberculosis, there was no other recourse than to turn to prayer. One evening Ellis and his wife, Claudius, stayed home from church and together with Oral's nurse circled his bed and began to pray. Oral remembers, "Lying there listening to Papa's earnest prayer and knowing he was praying because he loved me, I felt a warmth flow into my body." He adds, "As I looked, Papa's countenance changed in my sight. A bright light

FAITH

seemed to envelop him and suddenly the likeness of Jesus appeared in his face. I fell back on the pillow sobbing and crying, 'Jesus save me!' "

After some initial setbacks, Oral did recover, and joined his father in a new evangelistic ministry. They soon had more calls for revivals than they could handle, Ellis leading most of the preaching with his powerful voice and commanding style. Oral recalls, "I watched him and noticed how he loved me and encouraged me and finally asked me to preach every other night as we traveled."

By nineteen, Oral began preaching on his own in rural Oklahoma. After a few years of hardship in which he would often walk from town to town, the young, handsome, and aggressive Oral became well-known. In a five-week revival in Sand Springs, Oklahoma, church records show "fifty-two saved, nine sanctified, four received the Holy Ghost, nine baptized in water, twenty-six united with the church, and forty babies dedicated to God."

Roberts has become one of America's leading evangelists and faith healers. He founded Oral Roberts University in Tulsa in 1963. In 1960, when his father was ill and possibly near death, Roberts reportedly put his arm around him and said, "You can't die—I haven't told you about the University. I want you there when we dedicate it." The elder Roberts' eyes brightened, and he nearly shouted, "Praise the Lord." Ellis recovered, and after visiting the university in 1962 observed, "I think the new school is going to increase his ministry even more. I think that Oral's ministry is the winding up of the Gospel Age." In 1967, just before he died, Ellis asked his son to "win souls" in the funeral sermon Oral would soon give for him.

SOURCE:
Oral Roberts: An American Life, David Edwin Harrell Jr. (Indiana University Press, Bloomington, Indiana, 1985).

FAMOUS CHILD:	Susan B. Anthony
FATHER'S NAME:	Daniel Anthony

PAPA SAID: *"It would never do to have a woman overseer in the mill."*

*I*n 1820, Susan B. Anthony was born in Adams, Massachusetts. Her father, Daniel Anthony, was sent to a progressive Quaker boarding school by his parents, who were from a long line of Quakers. According to author Ilene Cooper, Daniel, "by the time he was a young man, had the reputation of following the 'inner light,' a Quaker term for a person's conscience." A man of principle, he frowned upon drinking, would not buy cotton for his mill that had been harvested by slaves, and in general believed in equality between men and women.

As progressive as his beliefs were for his time, however, Daniel stopped short of believing that a woman could hold a major and influential position in his cotton mill. At the cotton mill, there were several women employees. One, Sally Ann, excelled at weaving and was unequaled in her ability to maintain and repair the looms. One day Susan asked her father why, if Sally Ann was his most skilled employee, she wasn't the overseer. In response, Daniel said, "It would never do," igniting his young daughter's interest in women's rights.

Daniel raised his daughters to think for themselves and strongly supported their right to a good education at a time when many women were denied one. When Susan's male teacher decided that his female students did not need to learn long division, Daniel took both of his daughters out of the school and started one of his own by adding a room to a store he owned, offering evening classes for his mill workers as well.

Susan B. Anthony attended the first women's rights convention, in Seneca Falls, New York, in the summer of 1848. With a political belief similar to her father's, she fought not only for women's rights but also for the abolition of slavery and prohibition. With her friend Elizabeth Cady Stanton, Susan influenced generations of women.

In 1872, Susan B. Anthony was arrested for attempting to vote, insisting that the rights described in the Constitution should apply to women as well as men. She continued her work for the women's movement until her death at the age of eighty-six.

SOURCE:
Susan B. Anthony, Ilene Cooper (Franklin Watts, New York, 1984).

FAMOUS CHILD:	Ansel Adams
FATHER'S NAME:	Charles Adams

PAPA'S... *first commandment would have read, "Live each day bound by the highest moral standards as exemplified by the natural world."*

—*Mary Street Alinder*

charles Adams, referred to as Carlie by his son, was always a gentle and sensitive man. He read and reread the works of Ralph Waldo Emerson, who believed not in formal religion, but that all creatures belong to a larger soul and that the path to enlightenment could be obtained by living a principled life close to nature.

Ansel Adams was an only child and close to his parents. Their small house near the Lobos Creek in San Francisco overlooked the Golden Gate Bridge, and there Ansel explored nature, hunted driftwood, went clamming and crabbing, and spent happy days alone while developing a faith in the natural world similar to his father's. Ansel read voraciously, learned to read music, played the piano, and loved to be outdoors, but had difficulty in school and was eventually asked to leave his private school due to "inattention and misbehavior." According to author Mary Street Alinder, Ansel "today would be classified hyperactive, but then he was seen as a significant behavior problem."

By the time Ansel was thirteen, his father had suffered severe losses in his lumber business—fires and several shipwrecks—resulting in a more modest lifestyle for the family. Charles accepted a lower-paying job, but always cheered up when he saw his son. He and Ansel spent hours viewing the heavens with one of three telescopes they owned, and he always encouraged him to explore new opportunities, even though money was scarce. Ansel often watched his father take close-up photographs of flowers so that his mother could reproduce them in paint on china. Ansel became fascinated by photography, and on a trip to Yosemite National Park, fourteen-year old Ansel took pictures with his Box Brownie camera.

The Western landscape, the natural world, and specifically Yosemite fascinated Ansel Adams throughout his life. He returned there time and time again, often photographing the same view of El Capitan from Inspiration Point that he had taken as a teenager. By the time of his death in 1984, he was widely known as the most prominent photographer of the American landscape.

SOURCE:
Ansel Adams, Mary Street Alinder (Henry Holt, New York, 1996).

PERSPECTIVE

Joe Paterno
Martha Graham
Paul McCartney
Rush Limbaugh
Minnie Pearl
John James Audubon
E. B. White
Debbie Reynolds
Sally Ride
Gary Cooper
Edith Wharton
Lawrence Welk
Hugh Downs
John Travolta
Hank Aaron
Jerry Seinfeld
Joan Benoit Samuelson
Jay Leno

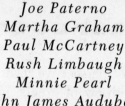   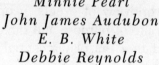   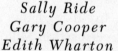   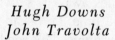   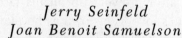

PERSPECTIVE

A good sense of perspective gives a person a clear and focused worldview of events, people, and choices. It helps a child lead a life of purpose and direction. By ways both subtle and overt, a father can play a central role in forming his child's view of the world.

One type of perspective that a father can give to a child is an educational or cultural perspective. Milton Downs tinkered with and built radios. Young Hugh was thrilled as he listened to a broadcast from 120 miles away. His "world" had gotten much bigger, and at the same time, he began to think of a future in radio. Charles Cooper introduced his son to his beloved American West. Years later, after growing up on his father's ranch, Gary transformed his dad's love to his own as he played western characters on the screen. Dale Ride didn't worry about household rules and discipline as long as his daughter was learning something. With her Ph.D. in hand, Sally Ride, the astronaut, grew up to explore the outer limits of space.

A father's humorous perspective allows his child to view life's challenges from a new angle—increasing the chance that he will pick himself up, brush himself off, and carry on when things get tough. Thomas Colley told story after story, as his eyes glistened with laughter. His daughter delighted in their telling, and after she grew up, Sarah Colley, as the lovable character Minnie Pearl, told stories herself for over fifty years at the Grand Ole Opry. Ray Reynolds was in a pickle. He couldn't find his family a home to rent—no one wanted kids. His satirical offer to "throw his kids away" after being denied yet again changed the prospective landlord's mind. Ray finally had a home for his family, as his daughter, Debbie, launched a life, and later a career, based on his positive and humorous outlook.

A father can also share a philosophical perspective that influences his child forever. Dr. George Graham, a keen observer of people, watched the way his patients moved and carried themselves. As a psychiatrist, he found these observations helpful. His daughter, dancer Martha Graham, made his fascination with movement her own and almost single-handedly invented the field of modern dance. Young Rush Limbaugh listened as his father and grandfather discussed current events. The men's conservative outlook later resurfaced in his life—Rush represents the third politically conservative generation in the Limbaugh family.

A father can also profoundly influence his child by "walking in his shoes" and, by doing so, seeing potential that a child may be too young to see for himself. Salvatore loved to watch his son act and observed that he was not only totally absorbed in the theater but talented as well. Allowing him to drop out of school at sixteen, Salvatore opened the door for his son's study of the theater and his subsequent success—John Travolta has been entertaining audiences ever since. Ludwig noticed that when his son milked the cows on the family farm, he did it in a rhythmic way. Realizing that his son might have talent, he encouraged him to take up the accordion, which his son, Lawrence Welk, used to create champagne music years later. Jean Audubon watched as his son struggled harder and harder at his lessons, while enjoying more and more the world of nature outside. Allowing him to leave school while encouraging his study of the natural world, Jean Audubon opened the door for John James Audubon's success as an artist and author. Audubon's drawings of birds have been celebrated worldwide.

The following stories celebrate this perspective. Each father has demonstrated an ability to see the big picture, greatly enhancing his child's life.

FAMOUS CHILD:	Joseph Vincent Paterno
FATHER'S NAME:	Angelo Lafayette Paterno

PAPA SAID: *"I've never made any real money, but I'm doing what I want to do. I think that's more important than money. If you like coaching, son, stay with it."*

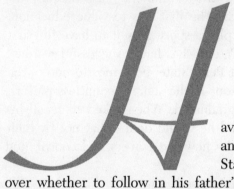

aving finished his first year as an assistant coach at Penn State, Joe Paterno struggled over whether to follow in his father's footsteps by going to law school or to remain on the sidelines. While the future coaching legend surmised that his mother already had him placed on a legal bench, Joe knew his father had the perspective to value the importance of doing what was important to you in making a career choice.

Angelo Paterno had played a key role in his son's development. At an early age, he taught Joe and his younger brother George the importance of honesty and helping each other. In a childhood incident that Paterno still recalls, Angelo made them face up to the situation the time they broke a large store window playing football. It was also his dad who decided to send his sons to Brown University instead of the more rigid moral environment of a Catholic university, prompting a warning from the local monsignor that "the boy's soul is in your hands."

Paterno credits his dad with two fundamental principles underlying his coaching success. The first was to value education. The second was that if you play a sport, play it to have fun first and to win second. While Paterno has had a successful win-loss record in over thirty years at Penn State, he is most proud of the many related intangible lessons he has taught countless players, 85 percent of whom have graduated. When asked to recall his most successful team, he said he would define that not by their win-loss record, but rather by how the players had contributed to society after college.

At the same time, Joe expressed regret that his father, who died in 1955 at fifty-eight, did not live to witness his success.

SOURCE:
Paterno by the Book, Joe Paterno with Bernard Asbell (Random House, New York, 1989).

FAMOUS CHILD:	Martha Graham
FATHER'S NAME:	Dr. George "Goldie" Graham

PAPA SAID: *"Each of us tells our own story, even without speaking. Movement never lies."*

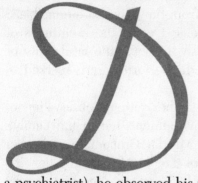

r. George "Goldie" Graham was a keen observer of people. As a successful "alienist" (today called a psychiatrist), he observed his patients, who he felt "moved and held themselves as they do for good reasons." With her father's office on the first floor of the family home, young Martha had ample opportunity to observe the comings and goings of her father's patients.

One evening, a woman came to dinner. The troubled young woman had poor posture. She didn't sit up straight and didn't look at anyone at the table. Later, young Martha asked her father why she carried herself so. Dr. Graham replied that the woman wasn't well emotionally, and her body was telling them this. "Each of us," Dr. Graham added, "tells our own story, even without speaking. Movement never lies."

At fourteen, Martha and her family moved from the industrial coal town of Allegheny, Pennsylvania, to Santa Barbara, California. Martha had always felt the "darkness" of Allegheny—its industry, its coal, and its winter climate. When she moved to Santa Barbara, she felt she had moved from the darkness into a "blaze of light." The sparkle of the Pacific Ocean, the multitudes of flowers, the beauty of the Spanish missions, the availability of silent movies, and the richness of the performing arts sparked an excitement in the young teen.

These two major perspectives—her father's observation of movement and the change in environment due to the family's relocation to California—poised Martha Graham to make her unique contribution to the field of dance. After seeing her first dance performance as a senior in high school—one by the celebrated Ruth St. Denis—the strong-willed and creative student focused on learning dance herself.

Accepted by a new school of dance, the Cumnock School of Expression in Los Angeles, the free-spirited young student rebelled against the traditional dance conventions and created a more contemporary style of her own—a style defined by her smooth agility, electrifying moves, and emotional expression. She very quickly stood out from the rest. Armed with her father's advice to "keep your soul open," and as a keen observer of movement, Martha readily interpreted dance with a creative flair that few before her had possessed.

It was while Martha was a second-year college student that her father died, never to ultimately see her career as a world-renowned dancer and choreographer. She went on to teach at the Eastman School of Music in Rochester, New York, ultimately opened her own studio in New York City in 1927, and the rest is dance history.

According to author Paula Bryant Pratt, Martha Graham tried to "show the trials of the human spirit, and the triumph over those trials." With a colorful perspective and a personal flair modeled by her father, Martha Graham and her individualistic interpretation of dance dominated the field for decades.

SOURCE:
The Importance of . . . Martha Graham, Paula Bryant Pratt (Lucent Books, San Diego, 1995).

FAMOUS CHILD:	Paul McCartney
	(James Paul McCartney)
FATHER'S NAME:	James McCartney

PAPA... *described the two "ations"—short for "toleration" and "moderation." He told his sons that if they were mindful of these two words, they would avoid hurting not only others, but themselves as well.*

efore Liverpool's citizens first heard of the Beatles, they may have heard Jim Mac's Jazz Band. The band's leader, James McCartney, may have been deaf in one ear, but he sure could play the piano. He taught himself to play on an old upright, for there wasn't any extra money in his family for lessons. His Liverpool neighborhood, where the family had lived for close to a hundred years, was tough. Somehow, however, music made a difference. By the age of ten James had his first job, operating the spotlight at the Liverpool Theatre Royal, and at fourteen he worked as a "sample boy" in the cotton industry, eventually becoming an inspector for the town's sanitation department.

PERSPECTIVE

Although young Paul was an eager student and received special privileges in school, his early studies of music were unsuccessful. He resisted studying piano while his friends were outside playing, and the discipline and dedication demanded by the director of St. Chad's Choir, off Penny Lane, prompted Paul to give up the instrument.

It wasn't until Paul's mother died when he was fourteen, devastating the close family, that Paul dove into experimenting with his first Zenith guitar. He found solace in playing the instrument, missing meals while immersing himself in his newfound discipline. Paul's brother, Mike, two years younger, described Paul's obsession with music as "lose a mother and find a guitar." Soon, the brothers were performing as the McCartney Brothers, influenced musically by the Everly Brothers, Fats Domino, and Elvis. Paul went on to perform alone after Mike was unable to overcome his stage fright.

Paul's father, alone after the death of his wife, committed himself to raising his sons, spending all of his free time cooking, cleaning, and fulfilling his role of both mother and father. Mike said years later, "We both owe him a lot. It would have been easy for him to have gone off getting drunk every night. But he didn't. He stayed home and looked after us."

In 1957, at a village gathering at the local parish church in Woolton, Paul McCartney met a young John Lennon in a casual meeting that would shape music for generations. John, guitarist and lead vocalist in a band, the Quarrymen, was impressed with Paul's ability not only to play the guitar but to tune it, a skill none of the Quarrymen possessed. Two weeks later, Paul paired up with John Lennon, and within three years they had written dozens of songs together, beginning a musical partnership that would last until the Beatles broke up in 1970.

Paul, describing his dad years later as his "strongest musical influence," went on to exhibit the elder McCartney's early lessons in toleration and moderation. With a musical and personal perspective learned from his father, Paul contributed to the music world a creativity, discipline, and pleasant demeanor that would inspire music lovers not only during his years with the Beatles, but also, with his post-Beatles band, Wings, through the seventies.

SOURCE:
Blackbird—The Life and Times of Paul McCartney, Geoffrey Giuliano (Dutton, New York, 1991).

FAMOUS CHILD:	Rush Limbaugh III
FATHER'S NAME:	Rush Limbaugh Jr.

PAPA SAID: *"Now why should I believe that?"*

T he outspoken radio talkmaster Rush Limbaugh III continues a strong family tradition of conservatism. Its roots originated with the broadcaster's grandfather, Rush Limbaugh Sr., who celebrated his centennial birthday in 1991 by continuing to practice law in the family's hometown of Cape Girardeau, Missouri, about a hundred miles south of St. Louis. He'd been given the name "Rush" by his maternal grandmother, Edna Rush, who was one of the area's original settlers shortly after the 1804 Louisiana Purchase.

Rush Junior, also a lawyer, was a Republican supporter in the 1950s and introduced candidate Richard Nixon to his town in a

1952 campaign visit. When his first son was born in 1951, he not only gave him the family name but also passed on to a third generation the conservative Limbaugh political perspective.

Paul D. Colford, author of a 1993 Limbaugh biography, states, "His father was his hero." While young "Rusty," as Rush III was called, exerted his independence by an early fascination with broadcasting—to the dismay of his father—he heard and accepted the family perspective on politics. Rush states, "I really think I learned more just from the times that we would sit down and talk and argue than I did any other way."

Family debate often centered on Rusty's difficulties at college, and reached a crescendo when he dropped out of the family alma mater, Southeast Missouri State University, in 1970 and eagerly devoted his efforts to radio. Colford states, "He finally rebelled against the father-knows-best, be-a-lawyer line, while adhering to the political views at his core." Eventually, when Rush returned home to Cape Girardeau for Rush Limbaugh III Day in 1989, he was at last a hero in his own hometown.

Rush's father finally joined the bandwagon following an appearance by Rush on Ted Koppel's *Nightline* show in 1990. The ailing, seventy-two-year-old man, impressed by his son's toughness and conservative commitment, asked his wife, "Where did he get that?"—to which the broadcaster's mom told the proud father, "He got it from you." When Rush's father died less than a month later, Rush eulogized him on his radio show, proud in the knowledge that he had indeed earned his father's respect, to go along with his unquestioned love.

SOURCE:
The Rush Limbaugh Story: Talent on Loan from God—An Unauthorized Biography, Paul D. Colford (St. Martin's Press, New York, 1993).

FAMOUS CHILD:	Minnie Pearl (Sarah Ophelia Colley)
FATHER'S NAME:	Thomas K. Colley

PAPA SAID: *"Remember, daughters, never let the truth interfere with a good story."*

innie Pearl, born Sarah Ophelia Colley in Centerville, Tennessee, in 1912, grew up in a close, conventional southern family headed by her father, Thomas, who owned and operated a lumber business with his father and brother. Minnie Pearl described her father as "a gentleman of the woods" and "a man of the earth" with the "soft-spoken dignity of Gary Cooper." According to Minnie Pearl, "I ran the house, which in truth meant I was spoiled." The family of five girls, of which she was the youngest, lived in a large gabled home with gingerbread trim and a wraparound porch that Minnie calls the "setting of many of the happiest memories of my life."

PERSPECTIVE

As a youngest daughter in a large family, Sarah Ophelia received much attention, leading to performances for family and friends on the piano at the age of four and to frequent demonstrations of dance and song. Thomas taught her to whistle and do birdcalls, and took her with him on horseback to visit the lumber camps he supervised. Throughout their childhood, Thomas told stories—incredible and extraordinary tales—that delighted and impressed his daughters, although they were "never real sure if he was telling the truth or not." One day young Sarah Ophelia exclaimed, "But, Daddy, that's not the way you told us the last time." "Well, of course it isn't," he responded. "Don't you like it better with something new added?" The talented storyteller was planting the seeds of creativity and perspective that his daughter, as Minnie Pearl, would reap many years later while entertaining others with stories of her own.

Sarah played the piano during silent films at a local theater, and after graduating from Ward-Belmont College she went on to teach, perform, and create the character "Minnie Pearl." The lovable, humorous, and enthusiastic Minnie Pearl related country anecdotes and stories based on people Sarah Ophelia had known while working and living as a young woman in an Alabama mountain village—all told in the local dialect. Later at home, demonstrating her character Minnie Pearl for her family in front of the fire, Sarah repeated her performance. Her father shared, "You'll make a fortune off that someday, Phel, if you keep it kind."

She did. With this wise advice passed on by her father, Sarah Ophelia Colley, as Minnie Pearl, joined the Grand Ole Opry in 1940 and performed regularly through the 1990s. Her father died and did not live to see his storytelling talents mirrored by his daughter, but Minnie Pearl states, "I've always tried to follow his advice and keep her kind."

SOURCE:
Minnie Pearl—An Autobiography, Minnie Pearl with Joan Dew (Pocket Books, New York, 1980).

FAMOUS CHILD: John James Audubon

FATHER'S NAME: Jean Audubon ("The Admiral")

PAPA SAID: *"Revolutions too often take place in the lives of individuals, and they are apt to lose in one day the fortune they before possessed; but talents and knowledge, added to sound mental training, assisted by honest industry, can never fail, nor be taken from any one once the possessor of such valuable means."*

John James Audubon, brought up in the midst of revolutionary France, studied at home with tutors hired by his father because of the volatile political climate. When formal learning became too difficult for him as a teenager, his father had the perspective to guide his creative son in other directions.

John spent hours when he wasn't being tutored at home hiking in fields and woods, fishing and hunting and finding birds' eggs, nests, and feathers, often bringing the treasures home to hang on his wall in his bedroom, which soon resembled a museum. Studies, however, were not quite as enjoyable for him. By the age of fourteen, Audubon found himself in a military academy, enrolled by his father, who was less than impressed with his son's academic efforts. One year later, the unhappy, creative boy, finding the structure of naval school too much to bear, attempted to escape.

Realizing that his son did not fit the traditional academic model, Jean Audubon acknowledged his son's creativity, allowed him to leave school, and encouraged him to expand his interest in natural history and drawing. Now free, John spent hours drawing in crayon and watercolor, having received a book from his father entitled *Illustrations* that inspired him to copy nature.

In 1803, eighteen-year-old John eventually moved to Mill Grove, a farm near Philadelphia along the Schuylkill River, which his father had bought to protect his assets during those turbulent times in France. With unusual energy, an emerging artistic interest, and a passion for birds, John James Audubon documented American bird life at Mill Grove, eventually expanding his goal to document and publish his drawings of all the birds in America. Later, with the support of his wife, Lucy, he traveled throughout the United States and Canada, finishing his book, *The Birds of America*, in 1838. John James Audubon called his father "an ingenious man to whom I owe all."

SOURCE:
Audubon—A Biography, John Chancellor (Viking Press, New York, 1978).

FAMOUS CHILD: E. B. White (Elwyn Brooks White)

FATHER'S NAME: Samuel Tilly White

PAPA SAID: *"If the time comes, as come it will, when you are fretted by the small things of life, remember that on this your birthday you heard a voice telling you to look up and out on the great things of life and beholding them say—surely they are all mine."*

Samuel White was keenly aware of the importance of his role as a father. His own had died prematurely in a home for "drunkards," propelling the young teen into a job as errand boy. Not one to bemoan his fate, Samuel by the age of thirty-two had not only put in thirteen years with the same company but was also one of its major stockholders. Determined to give his children all the things he'd lacked as a child, Samuel White filled his home with musical instruments and merry Christmases, while taking much pride in his country and his family. His advice was written to E. B. White on the occasion of the boy's twelfth birthday.

As a child, E. B. White religiously kept a diary and remembered the "noisy excitement" of the family's Oliver typewriter that had "encouraged him to be a writer," as had "looking at a square sheet of paper square in the eyes" and thinking, "This is where I belong. This is it." With the perspective of his father, who had survived a difficult childhood and had learned to appreciate both his professional and personal successes, E. B. White graduated from Cornell, wrote for *The New Yorker* magazine with his friend James Thurber, and penned the perennial favorites *Charlotte's Web* and *Trumpet of the Swan*, while often using his childhood journal as a reference upon which to embellish the stories.

After a long and successful literary career, E. B. White refers to another perspective that he may have learned from his father. His decision to be a writer may have been inspired by seeing his father "tied down and harried by business." E. B. White describes his years in Maine in the early forties, immortalized in *Charlotte's Web*, as "just about the best period in my life."

SOURCE:
E. B. White—A Biography, Scott Elledge (W. W. Norton, New York, 1984).

FAMOUS CHILD:	Debbie Reynolds
	(Mary Frances Reynolds)
FATHER'S NAME:	Ray Reynolds

PAPA SAID: *"I'm gonna take 'em out and drown 'em in the Los Angeles River tonight and come back tomorrow."*

It had been a real struggle to get his family to L.A., but Ray Reynolds' steady job as a carpenter with the railroad had made it possible. After almost a year and after his sending so much money home to Texas each week that he had to sleep on a bench in MacArthur Park, Ray's family stepped off the train. From one motel to another they wandered, looking for a place to stay until they could find a house, but the answer was always the same: No kids allowed. Ray couldn't help it; the words just slipped out of his mouth. Debbie adds, "She [the landlady] must have had the same sense of humor: We moved in the next day."

It had always been tough. When Mary Frances came home

from the hospital as an infant, the young family lived behind a gas station in two rooms, shared a rest room with the station's patrons, and cooked over a hot plate in a neighborhood full of boarded-up buildings. Her father's job—he was a car mechanic and handyman—brought him only a dollar a day in wages in the dust and dirt of hot and windy El Paso. About the only escape the quiet and gentle Ray Reynolds had was his love for baseball and a sense of humor. "I could usually get around my father by making him laugh," Debbie remembers.

With a lot of hard work and secondhand furnishings, Ray and the family moved into a small house in Burbank, not far from the Warner Brothers Studio. Debbie Reynolds recalls that the family had very little money but that she now had her very own room, a bathroom used by only four people, a place to go bowling, a neighborhood full of children, and "more food than I'd ever seen in Texas."

When she learned at sixteen that she could win a blouse and a scarf by entering the 1948 Miss Burbank contest, she signed right up. Off she went with borrowed high heels that were too big, with Kleenex stuffed in their toes; a bathing suit with a sewed-up hole in it; and a hastily put together Betty Hutton act that turned into a comedy routine onstage and broke up the audience. She not only won the contest, but got a free lunch, a string of pearls, an all-expenses-paid trip for two to New York

City, and a call from Warner Brothers Studio the next day asking her to screen-test.

Debbie took her father's humorous perspective and added it to her sparkling personality to create a legend in movies, television, nightclubs, and the theater. She appeared in *Singin' in the Rain*, *How the West Was Won*, and *The Unsinkable Molly Brown* during the Golden Age of Hollywood.

SOURCE:
Debbie—My Life, Debbie Reynolds and David Patrick Columbia (William Morrow, New York, 1988).

FAMOUS CHILD: Sally Kristen Ride

FATHER'S NAME: Dale Ride

PAPA SAID: *"We might have encouraged, but mostly we let them explore."*

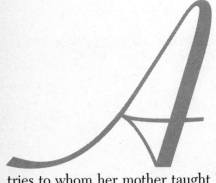

nd explore Sally did—learning about people through the many visitors from other countries to whom her mother taught English, and searching intellectually through books and newspapers. Dale Ride taught political science at Santa Monica College, and during her father's sabbatical in Europe when she was nine, Sally and her sister climbed around castles, walked through centuries-old cities, and learned still more about the world. The busy household encouraged accomplishment while not a lot of attention was spent on chores, meals, or housework. According to author Carolyn Blacknall, this gave the Ride family time to "try out new things and ideas."

With this perspective—one much larger than merely her home and neighborhood in southern California—Sally Ride stood ready to achieve greater heights. After nine years of study at Swarthmore College and Stanford University, Sally was about to earn her doctoral degree in astrophysics when she noticed an ad for astronauts in the school paper. She was eventually one of only thirty-five astronauts picked out of a field of more than eight thousand applicants.

On June 18, 1983, astronaut Sally Ride took off aboard the space shuttle orbiter *Challenger* and solidly placed herself in the history books as America's first woman in space. Witnessing the event along with millions of others were her family, government officials, and feminists Jane Fonda and Gloria Steinem.

After the flight, NASA's director of flight operations, George Abbey, said, "You get people who can sit in the lab and think like an Einstein, but they can't do anything with it. Sally can get everything she knows together and bring it to bear where you need it." That's perspective.

SOURCE:
Sally Ride—America's First Woman in Space, Carolyn Blacknall (Dillon Press, Minneapolis, 1984).

FAMOUS CHILD:	Gary Cooper (Frank James Cooper)
FATHER'S NAME:	Charles Cooper
PAPA SAID:	*"Well, son, I'll see what I can do to help you."*

Charles Cooper was excited. After having grown up in England, he had moved to the United States, become a citizen, and now lived on a ranch in Montana—right in the middle of the American West that he had always loved from afar. He had cattle, horses, ranch hands to help him, a wife, two sons—five-year-old Frank James and his older brother—and was studying law on the side. Soon he would earn the title of judge.

Frank James Cooper lived among the cowhands and the neighboring Indians, who went with him to the ranch school his father had started. He rode horses, explored the pastures and woods, and learned a lot about life. This was much more fun than school. According to author Larry Swindell, as Frank grew older he earned the title of "Judge Cooper's Wild Kid," playing practical jokes and carousing with his friends. It took a transfer to a new high school and a special program orchestrated by his father and the principal to get him past graduation.

He struggled at Grinnell College in Iowa, where his favorite course was drawing and he sketched as often as he could. He tried out for a few parts in college plays, with little success. He worked several summers at Yellowstone National Park as a tour guide. Nothing concrete came out of any of it until he dropped out of college and rather impulsively went to Hollywood in 1924 looking for a movie career, while he explained to his conservative dad that he was going to pursue an art career.

That's when things started to happen. He landed in the dawn of the movie age—silent movies had just been introduced to an eager American audience. Now he had to tell his father about his plans. During a brief visit to San Diego, they met. Frank explained that he knew he had been a disappointment to him, especially in his choice of careers, but that his future looked bright in the movies. He didn't want financial support; he only wanted his parents' moral support.

Charles Cooper, a man who had left his own birthplace to pursue a love of the American West, saw before him a son who had traveled to Hollywood hoping to translate that American West to a movie screen. Their perspective couldn't be that different, he figured. After a sincere statement of support, Charles contacted a friend, Colonel Ford, who was a production manager in the movie industry, and Ford subsequently gave Frank Cooper his first leading role, in a new western, *Lightnin' Wins*.

From parts as a "riding extra" in westerns to walk-ons, and then as a handsome and debonair leading man, the young Frank James Cooper became Gary Cooper, and with the change in name came the beginning of his legendary career. He appeared in many major films from 1928 to 1957, receiving Academy Awards for *Sergeant York* in 1941 and *High Noon* in 1952.

SOURCE:
The Last Hero—A Biography of Gary Cooper, Larry Swindell (Doubleday, New York, 1980).

FAMOUS CHILD:	Edith Wharton
FATHER'S NAME:	George Frederic Jones

PAPA... *"lived through his eyes, as his daughter would later."*
—*Eleanor Dwight*

George Frederic Jones loved to travel, and with the generous income from his inheritance, he could travel in style as well as live a life of leisure when he finally returned home. After the end of the Civil War, he and his family spent six years in Europe. He drank in and remembered everything he saw as he and his daughter walked Renaissance garden paths, visited art galleries, studied classical architecture, and experienced festivals in Rome. He described his travels in a diary that became alive with verbal images.

Raised as an only child, since her brothers had long ago left home, Edith grew up in New York City and spent summers among the wealthy of Newport in between travels. The creative child drank in the beauty of her father's Europe, and when she was an adult the memories remained so vivid that they could be retrieved at the touch of her pen to paper. She spent hours at home writing stories and observing the comings and goings at the Fifth Avenue Hotel, the center of the city's social and political life, directly across the street from her four-and-a-half-story brownstone. She retreated to her father's library, where, in privacy, she could explore its many volumes, finding those she called her "friends" between the pages.

As a teenager, Edith had poems published in both a New York newspaper and in *The Atlantic Monthly*; several of them were admired by Henry Wadsworth Longfellow. Her 1920 novel, *The Age of Innocence*, received a Pulitzer Prize and was made into a 1993 film of the same name. *Ethan Frome* and *House of Mirth*, among other works, also achieved significant literary success. Often describing him as her "soul mate," Edith Wharton shared her father's love of the world, and like him, just had to write it down.

Her father was "stricken by paralysis" and subsequently died in 1882, and she wrote years later of being "still haunted by the look in his dear blue eyes, which had followed me so tenderly for nineteen years, and now tried to convey the goodbye messages he could not speak. I doubt if life holds a subtler anguish."

SOURCE:
Edith Wharton—An Illustrated Biography, Eleanor Dwight (Harry N. Abrams, New York, 1994).

FAMOUS CHILD:	Lawrence Welk
FATHER'S NAME:	Ludwig Welk
PAPA SAID:	*"Dummer Esel!* Can't you do anything right?"

T he future maker of champagne music was not cut out to be a farmer. His German immigrant father quickly figured this out as young Lawrence was unable to effectively pump the bellows on his blacksmith's forge, refused to butcher the hogs, and irritated the cows by trying to milk them in rhythm.

Ludwig had not brought many possessions with him from Germany to North Dakota, but his accordion was one of them. Loving music himself, he had the perspective to see an innate musical ability in his son's rhythmic attempts at milking. He advanced him $400 to buy a piano accordion if Lawrence would agree to stay on the farm for four more years and turn over to him all the money he made by playing barn dances and wedding parties.

Lawrence kept his end of the bargain. On his twenty-first birthday, in 1924, he took the accordion, a prayer book, and his parents' blessings and set out on the road to begin his music career with the Lincoln Boulds traveling band in Estherville, Iowa. He kept moving on, eventually forming Welk's Novelty Band, which acquired a regular show on a Yankton, South Dakota, radio station beamed over a four-hundred-mile radius. In 1955, with his champagne music style fully developed and with his family of musicians, Welk began a sixteen-year tenure as a Saturday night TV fixture on ABC.

Welk credits his father's early perspective for his eventual success, stating, "I've always been very grateful for his decision, because I know how very worried he was for fear I'd lose my faith, in the rough-and-tumble world of show business."

SOURCE:
Lawrence Welk's Musical Family Album, Lawrence Welk with Bernice McGeehan (Prentice-Hall, Englewood Cliffs, New Jersey, 1977).

FAMOUS CHILD:	Hugh Downs
FATHER'S NAME:	Milton Downs
PAPA SAID:	*"That voice is coming from Cincinnati!"*

S even-year-old Hugh was fascinated by the vacuum tubes and batteries hooked up to a large speaker dangling above the radio that his father made. Hearing a 1928 broadcast from Cincinnati, 120 miles away from their home in Lima, Ohio, was truly magic. Hugh Downs recalls, "At that age, I probably didn't grasp what the distance meant. I just knew it was nowhere nearby." This small vision, however, became the foundation for a worldwide perspective for the host of ABC's *20/20*.

Broadcaster Hugh Downs was always intrigued by radio. Both were born in the early 1920s; Downs was born in Akron, Ohio, in 1921, not too far from Pittsburgh, where the first commercial radio broadcast took place on KDKA in 1920. His father inspired Hugh's interest in radio-related matters by demonstrating basic concepts like wave transmission over string tied between two spoons and voice transmission between two tin cans over a piece of wire. By the age of ten, Hugh was playing with a little do-it-yourself telephone transmitter. He later admitted, "My father's contagious interest in voice transmission may have led to my lifelong fascination with the idea of professional broadcasting."

Downs' formal broadcasting career started in 1939 when, inexperienced but interested, he walked into a Lima radio station and offered his services. A combination of luck and managerial perspective intervened. Despite a sound test which was classified by the station manager as "really quite bad," the manager added, "Great oaks from little acorns grow," and offered Hugh a job for $12.50 a week. Milton Downs was not thrilled with his son's radio prospects, and suggested that he "keep looking for a job for a week. If you don't find a job, go with the radio station."

After Hugh took the job, his dad provided an additional perspective on broadcasting: "Just stop and think that people have dials on their radios. If they don't like what you are saying, they can tune to some other station." Few did. Hugh Downs' broadcasting career flourished, and he is now listed in the *Guinness Book of World Records* as having logged the most hours in history on network television.

SOURCE:
On Camera—My 10,000 Hours on Television, Hugh Downs (G. P. Putnam's Sons, New York, 1986).

FAMOUS CHILD:	John Travolta
FATHER'S NAME:	Salvatore Travolta

PAPA SAID: *"You can leave school for a year—and if everything works out and you can make money, you won't have to go back."*

It's always difficult when a child suggests dropping out of high school, but Salvatore Travolta, owner of the Travolta Tire Exchange in Englewood, New Jersey, was just positive that his son had a mission in the arts. Without his father's perspective, John Travolta might have been just another high school hotshot instead of the television and movie idol he became—from *Welcome Back, Kotter* to *Grease*, *Saturday Night Fever*, and *Pulp Fiction*.

The youngest of six children, John was adored by his parents, who treasured their late-in-life gift. Acting had always been a love for Travolta growing up, and he was supported by a talented family that valued entertainment. His mother was a former actress who worked as a drama teacher, while his two brothers and three sisters were involved in the performing arts as well. They all honed their talents in nightly family sketches, song-and-dance routines, and minidramas.

John, who took tap-dancing lessons from Gene Kelly's brother, was more interested in performing than in studying. He admitted, "I was a bit of a clown in school, only an average student." Salvatore Travolta, in comparing his son's extraordinary talent with his most ordinary school performance, opened the door to John's success.

SOURCES:

The John Travolta Scrapbook, Suzanne Munshower (Sunridge Press, New York, 1976).

"A Star Reborn: The Rise and Fall and Rise of John Travolta," Michael Segell, *Cosmopolitan*, January 1996, Volume 220, No. 1.

John Travolta, Current Biography, #39 (H. W. Wilson, New York, 1978).

FAMOUS CHILD:	Henry "Hank" Aaron
FATHER'S NAME:	Herbert Aaron

PAPA SAID: *"Nobody wanted to hear what I had to say until I proved myself."*

During Hank Aaron's baseball career, he listened to his father's advice and, busy as he was hitting a record 755 home runs, let his bat do his talking. He remembers the racist remarks and taunts he had to endure during his minor-league years in the early 1950s and even after he made it to the major leagues in 1954. Hank says that one reason blacks did so well in the early years was that "we had to. There was too much at stake for us to screw it up." While his critics have said that he might have been a more vocal spokesperson against racism earlier in his career, Hank counters that, claiming, "Until I became the guy with the chance to break Babe Ruth's record, the mainstream media just didn't care what I had to say."

Hank viewed his father as someone with the perspective to *go* along in order to *get* along. Herbert Aaron was a boilermaker's assistant on dry docks, holding sixty-pound steel plates while someone else riveted them into ships. He also operated a tavern and did odd jobs to make ends meet. Although a small town baseball player all his life and sympathetic with his son's desire to play, he was more concerned about selling refreshments to make money for the team. Quiet-spoken, the elder Aaron preached the value of respect to his children. Sometimes the respect was earned; sometimes it was just common sense. Henry recalled that with a houseful of kids to feed, Herbert could ill afford confrontations. "He would say all the right things and go along with the system, despite what he might have thought deep down."

Aaron, now retired and enshrined in baseball's Hall of Fame, has become a more active spokesperson for equal rights in baseball. His 1991 book, *I Had a Hammer*, is an outspoken statement of his experience in dealing with racism. Media magnate Ted Turner observes the change, noting that Aaron "breaks [his] silence with quiet dignity, strength of character, and pride—qualities synonymous with an American legend." And that, thanks to the perspective that Herbert Aaron taught his son, is just what Hank Aaron is.

SOURCE:
I Had a Hammer—The Hank Aaron Story, Hank Aaron with Lonnie Wheeler (HarperCollins, New York, 1991).

FAMOUS CHILD:	Jerry Seinfeld
FATHER'S NAME:	Kalman Seinfeld

PAPA SAID: *"Sometimes I don't even care if I get the order, I just have to break that face."*

*F*or Kal Seinfeld, the owner of a Long Island sign company, a good laugh started with the name of his business—the Kal Signfeld Sign Company. While his customers usually only wanted a simple and straightforward sign such as PHIL'S COLOR TV, Kal's goal was to "break their face" and make them laugh.

Jerry accompanied his dad on his travels about Long Island in his pickup truck, watching as he negotiated with the serious, task-oriented businessmen. As Kal went about his rounds, he would grab any humor he could in the course of the day, inspiring Jerry to say, "There has never been a professional comedian with better stage presence, attitude, timing, or delivery."

PERSPECTIVE

While Jerry loved to watch his dad work and was most influenced by the humorous perspective of his father, he also was inspired by television comedians Bill Cosby and Alan King. Not only did Jerry have all of Bill Cosby's comedy albums, but he also followed his example by wearing sneakers most of the time, as he still does. Young Jerry's home-based classroom of comedy had such teaching aides as *The Ed Sullivan Show* on television and such comic book heroes as *Batman*, *Spiderman*, and *Superman*. Later he went off to Queens College, where he graduated with a B.A. in 1976.

In his television comedy series, *Seinfeld*, Jerry, in his own words, takes "the most normal things in life and spends way too much time thinking about them," as his millions of fans watch. Impressed that his book, *SeinLanguage*, is in the bookstores, Jerry adds, "A bookstore is one of the only pieces of physical evidence we have that people are still thinking."

SOURCE:
SeinLanguage, Jerry Seinfeld (Bantam Books, New York, 1993).

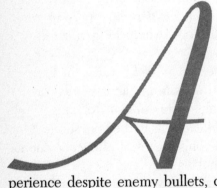

ndre Benoit served in the ski troops during World War II and survived the dangerous experience despite enemy bullets, cold, and avalanches. After the war, while he encouraged his daughter Joan and his three sons in their athletic pursuits, he always promoted two important athletic perspectives as well—have fun, and do it safely.

He exposed Joan to skiing at age three, and it wasn't long before she was an accomplished skier, with a dream of a professional career. A leg injury at fifteen, however, put an end to this dream. Then, as she ran to recover leg strength, she found her calling. She explains, "Because I ran and played other sports,

I could give up competitive skiing; running was compensation."

   She joined a regional cross-country running club that ran in meets throughout Maine. Her father, who now operated a Benoit family clothing store, would get up early in the morning to take her to her running group. He often wondered why she would want to mix in this time-consuming activity with an already busy high school schedule. When he asked if she was having fun at it, Joan shared her love for running while encouraging him to try it himself. She notes that he took her advice and has been running ever since.

   It wasn't long before Joan was running and winning major races and eventually marathons. Her most notable moment came when she won the first-ever women's marathon event at the 1984 Olympics in Los Angeles. Upon her parents' return to their Maine home after the event, they found that friends had decorated their house with a gold medal and the words, "It all started here."

SOURCE:
Running Tide, Joan Benoit with Sally Baker (Alfred A. Knopf, New York, 1987).

FAMOUS CHILD: Jay Leno (James Douglas Leno)
FATHER'S NAME: Angelo Leno
PAPA SAID: *"You just fight the good fight, son."*

ay Leno listened to his dad and did indeed fight the good fight. The man who inherited what he calls the "biggest gig in the world" from Johnny Carson on *The Tonight Show* in 1992 got there the hard way. He had begun his climb to fame more than twenty years earlier, as an Emerson College undergraduate who did stand-up comedy in Boston bars to earn money.

Jay grew up in Andover, Massachusetts, where his Italian-American father was an insurance salesman. Dad, too, was known for his sense of humor, often serving as a joke-telling master of ceremonies at insurance company meetings and banquets. "I just assumed I'd always be some sort of gregarious salesman who knew a joke to emcee birthday parties," said Leno in proclaiming his admiration for his dad. He adds that he was happy as a child and says his upbringing provided the perspective that underlies his sense of humor, which has been characterized as being "delivered without malice."

Jay was a prankster as a child. One high school prank he admits to was pouring water into a Kotex machine and watching the machine come apart as the napkins absorbed water. After high school, Jay went to college, his parents' advice in mind: "Finish college, get your degree, and you can always teach if you can't find something else." Biographer Bill Adler observes, "Resounding support for a show-biz career it was not." He adds, "Leno grew up lucky, with loving parents and lots of friends—requisites for a decent, healthy outlook on life." He has carried that outlook into the popular monologues and comedy routines he performs on *The Tonight Show*.

One of his most poignant moments came shortly after his father died. Directly facing the camera, Leno delivered a riveting eight-minute eulogy in which he shared a fundamental perspective. "Losing two parents in one year is a pretty tricky thing to take. When I heard the expression 'It's lonely at the top' I never knew what it meant. I had no idea, because at every point along the way, they were there for me to talk to."

SOURCES:

The World of Jay Leno, Bill Adler and Bruce Cassiday (Carol Publishing Group, New York, 1992).

"Leno Lives," Bill Zehme, *Esquire*, October 1995, Volume 124, No. 4.

RESPONSIBILITY

Arthur Ashe
Roberto Clemente
Pablo Casals
Jane Addams
Bill Bradley
Clara Barton
Benjamin Franklin
George Burns
Bernard Baruch
Gordie Howe
Charlton Heston
Walt Disney
Wilbur and Orville Wright
John Studebaker
Lawrence "Yogi" Berra
Trisha Yearwood

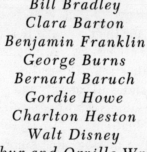

RESPONSIBILITY

*F*athers who foster responsibility in their children guide them to take charge of their lives, to answer for their conduct, and to account for their actions. Responsible people make better decisions. Better decisions make better people. Twentieth-century American author J. G. Holland describes a responsibility that "walks hand in hand with capacity and power." The following stories celebrate the fathers who passed these gifts of "capacity and power" to their children.

When a child gets a message that emphasizes social or political responsibility, more people may benefit than just those in the child's immediate neighborhood. Jane Addams was proud of her new coat, and couldn't wait to wear it to Sunday school. Her father, while agreeing that it was indeed beautiful, suggested that she not wear it, for it might make the less fortunate girls feel bad. Jane Addams grew up and started a settlement house in Chicago that aided, housed, and educated the poor. Carlos Casals always believed that governments should be free and that they should support working people. His son, Pablo, played to audiences around the world as a cellist while refusing to play in countries with oppressive governments, and before the onset of World War II he encouraged Spain not to participate in the 1936 Olympics in Germany. Captain Stephen Barton always made it a point to give to the poor and was instrumental in founding a home for destitute families in his town. Later, his daughter, Clara, pleaded with Colonel Daniel Rucker to allow her to bring supplies to the front during the Civil War. By 1881, Clara Barton had started the American Red Cross.

The father who models financial responsibility for his child gives the child a pragmatic and practical foundation upon which to build a successful life and career. Work hard, honor your debts and pay them: simple advice, but often necessary advice if a child wants to get ahead. Elias Disney was a down-to-earth and practical man. His son needed his job at the jelly factory—after all, it paid twenty-five dollars a week. Walt had other ideas. He and his brother wanted to start the Disney Brothers Studio, and needed $2,500 to do it. Reluctantly, his dad said yes, and with Walt Disney's financial common sense and propensity for hard work—qualities he'd inherited from his father—he went on to turn the $2,500 into a fortune—but not before promising his dad that someday the name "Disney" would be known around the world. John Studebaker had a sign over his blacksmith shop: OWE NO MAN ANYTHING BUT TO LOVE ONE ANOTHER. When times got tough, he relocated his family to seek better opportunities while struggling to keep his business afloat, and he managed to pay his debtors. Not many years later, two of his sons, and then three of their brothers, started a successful automobile manufacturing company.

When a father passes along to his child a moral message, the child never forgets. Warren Bradley was proud indeed. He was a small-town banker and as such knew and was trusted by most of the people in his community. The Depression was tough, but never once did he have to foreclose on a home. As a United States senator, Bill Bradley tried to view issues from both sides of the aisle. Jack Kemp said, "Anyone who loves the country should take a look at it through Bill Bradley's eyes." Behind those eyes are the values from his Midwestern childhood.

Nineteenth-century Scottish author George MacDonald said, "The best preparation for the future is the present well seen to, the last duty well done." If so, these fathers prepared their children well.

FAMOUS CHILD:	Arthur Robert Ashe Jr.
FATHER'S NAME:	Arthur Robert Ashe Sr.

PAPA SAID: *"What people think of you, Arthur Junior, your reputation is all that counts."*

Future tennis star Arthur Ashe was born in Virginia and named after his father, an eighth-generation African-American. Arthur Senior became both mother and father to six-year-old Arthur Junior and his brother when his wife died at age twenty-seven. While only semiliterate, the elder Ashe worked as a special policeman, caterer, cook, waiter, and groundskeeper to support his family. It was during his job as a tennis court supervisor in Richmond that his son was first exposed to tennis, when the court professional, Ron Charity, asked the seven-year-old if he would like to learn the game. While Charity and others helped young Arthur develop the skills that eventually led him to his position of captain of the United States Davis Cup team, it was his father who helped him develop his character.

Ashe recalled in his autobiography that he was once asked why no one ever seemed to say anything bad about him, to which he replied, "I guess I have never misbehaved because I'm afraid that if I ever did anything like that, my father would come straight up from Virginia, find me wherever I happen to be, and kick my ass."

Ashe noted that his father, who died in 1989, was a strong, dutiful, and providing man who built his own home from highway department scrap materials discarded in the construction of an interstate road. He recalled that the lesson his father taught him "above all was about reputation."

This became even more important in 1988, when Ashe was diagnosed as having AIDS as a result of a blood transfusion following a heart-bypass operation years before. During the last five years of his life, Ashe dedicated himself to such issues as AIDS and racial injustice. In a touching letter written just before his death in 1993 to his then seven-year-old daughter, Camera, Ashe noted the discrimination faced by his father in the South after World War I and the strength he'd required to work through it. He noted in particular a family tree painted by a cousin, and noted that this tree, like the one referred to by Maya Angelou in her 1992 presidential inauguration poem, stood for "family, both immediate and extended." He asked Camera to remember that the tree's keys to survival were the strength and depth of its roots, which not only gave it life but which would help it sway and bend but not break in times of trouble. He concluded the thought with, "You must never forget your place on that tree."

SOURCE:
Days of Grace: A Memoir, Arthur Ashe and Arnold Rampersad (Alfred A. Knopf, New York, 1993).

FAMOUS CHILD:	Roberto Clemente
FATHER'S NAME:	Melchor Clemente

PAPA SAID: *"I want you to become a good man, a serious man."*

*M*elchor and Luisa Clemente raised seven children in a little square white house in a poor area of the small town of San Anton near San Juan, Puerto Rico. The family was poor but, according to a friend, "They were cultured people—not sophisticated, just good people who did right by others." According to Clemente's biographer, Phil Musick, Melchor believed: "A man paid his debts, accorded and demanded respect, carried himself with dignity, provided for his own, assisted the less fortunate."

Roberto's obsession with baseball started at age five. A ready and inexpensive supply of baseballs was obtained by crumpling magazine pages into round balls. When times got a little better for his father, he would give Roberto an occasional quarter for the bus trip to San Juan to watch the San Juan Senators in the Puerto Rican winter league. Roberto's mother wanted him to study more and to someday become an engineer, but his father became impressed with Roberto's baseball skills after watching him hit ten home runs in a seven-hour sandlot game. Melchor offered the compromise that his son play baseball and study later, and he eventually signed a contract with the Brooklyn Dodgers for his seventeen-year-old son.

In 1970, Melchor Clemente joined his son in Pittsburgh. Described by a sportswriter as a "tired eagle," the proud ninety-year-old man from Puerto Rico watched his son play the sport of his youth. Several years later, Roberto Clemente got his three thousandth hit on the last day of the 1972 season. It was to be his last. On New Year's Eve of 1973, the thirty-eight-year-old baseball star with four batting titles was killed in a plane crash.

Roberto Clemente always demonstrated a responsibility to his community and its needs—much like his dad's responsibility to the needy of Puerto Rico. It was ironic that Roberto was killed in a plane crash on which he, as honorary chairman of the Nicaraguan Relief Committee, was helping bring food and supplies to earthquake-ravaged Nicaragua. He'd developed a special connection to Nicaragua, where he managed in a winter league and arranged for artificial legs for a young boy who'd had both his legs amputated.

Roberto's memory was honored in many ways, from Pittsburgh to San Juan. One schoolchild may have summed him up best by her response to her teacher's question, "Why should the world remember Roberto Clemente?" She replied, "He cared enough. He didn't care if he died; all he knew was that he tried."

SOURCE:
Who Was Roberto? A Biography of Roberto Clemente, Phil Musick (Doubleday, New York, 1994).

FAMOUS CHILD:	Pablo Casals (Pablo Carlos Salvador Casals y Defillo)
FATHER'S NAME:	Carlos Casals

PAPA... *first encouraged young Pablo in his music but then argued that "a career in music was too risky because only the very best could make a living at it."*

orn in 1876, Pablo Casals grew up hearing organ music and the sound of a church choir through the walls of his home next to the village church in Vendrell, near Barcelona, Spain. His father was the church organist and choirmaster and taught piano in the parlor downstairs. Pablo sang before he spoke and with his unusual musical talent played several instruments and was composing music by the age of seven. He was entertained regularly by the town's roaming street musicians and the town fishermen as they went about their work, and author Hedda Garza writes that Pablo also spent summers on a San Salvador beach where "the sound of waves combined with the squawking of the gulls and whistling of the wind created music in his head."

Pablo Casals' broad interest in music became much more focused once his father created an instrument out of a dried gourd in his workshop. This new sound fascinated the young musician, and soon after, when he heard a similar but richer sound—the mellow sound of a cello—he knew where his interest in music would take him. By the time he was twelve, everyone knew that Pablo Casals would make the mastery of the cello his lifelong career.

This concerned the pragmatic Carlos, who made his opinion known: that only the very best musicians made a decent living and that therefore Pablo should apprentice as a carpenter—a career which would promise a regular paycheck. Carlos had spent his own musical career struggling to support his family and was determined that his son should not meet the same fate. At this point, Pablo's mother successfully intervened and convinced her husband that Pablo should study music in Barcelona. After only five years of study, at the age of fifteen, Pablo Casals gave his first concert, demonstrating a genius that the world would continue to witness throughout his long career.

While performing throughout the world, Pablo Casals integrated a political philosophy learned from his father: a philosophy of liberal, free, and representative government that championed the rights of working people. According to Garza, Pablo Casals "believed that people of conscience, particularly those of international stature, had a duty to take a public stand against political oppression in all forms, and he refused to play in countries where oppressive governments committed brutal crimes against humanity." Denouncing the activities of the Nazi movement in Germany, he encouraged Spain to boycott the 1936 Olympics and to schedule its own Olympic event at home. Pablo also desired that the poorest children should have access to music, and championed music programs in the public schools.

In the 1930s, as the Spanish Republic crumbled, Pablo Casals became an artist-in-exile to protest the Fascist regime of Francisco Franco, performing in the greatest concert halls throughout the world as well as for coal miners in Wilkes-Barre, Pennsylvania. He was still recording for Columbia Records past the age of seventy—while still being described as the "greatest cellist in the world." Then and before, Pablo Casals echoed the musical and political teachings he'd learned from his father many years before.

SOURCE:
Pablo Casals, Hedda Garza (Chelsea House Publishers, New York, 1993).

FAMOUS CHILD: Jane Addams

FATHER'S NAME: John Addams

PAPA SAID: *"It's a very pretty cloak—in fact, much prettier than any cloak the other little girls in the Sunday school have. Wear your old cloak; it will keep you quite warm, with the added advantage of not making the other little girls feel badly."*

*J*ane Addams, from Cedarville, Illinois, lost her mother at the age of two and spent her early years with her father, John. An early settler in the former Indian Territory, he supported expansion of the railroad and ran for office extensively, eventually winning the race for Illinois Republican state senator. John's political activities brought him friendship with Abraham Lincoln, whom he supported in the effort to free the slaves. John both organized and equipped a contingent of Cedarville soldiers to support the Civil War effort. When Jane was four and a half years old, Lincoln was assassinated, and for the first time, according to author Cornelia Meigs, "she saw her father in tears."

Jane Addams claimed that her father and his values were the dominant influence of her childhood. During one sleepless night as a child, Jane Addams confessed to her father that she had told a lie. His response? If he had "a little girl who told lies," he was very glad that she felt "too bad to go to sleep afterward."

After her father died, and just after her graduation from Rockford Female Seminary in Illinois, Jane entered eight years of struggle, aimless travel, and profound unhappiness. While in London, Jane discovered Toynbee Hall, where educated young women could live with and help the city's poor. The founder believed that one could best help the needy by living among them as an equal. This sense of social responsibility, not wholly different from the one her father obviously felt, inspired her to reach out of her despair and grasp a goal—the institution of a "settlement house," which she and her friend, Ellen Starr, brought to one of the poorest neighborhoods of Chicago.

They founded Hull House in 1889 in a West Side Chicago slum that was densely populated and full of children. It served immigrants who worked in the stockyards, garment industry, factories, and sweatshops. Young college-educated women were hired, and they started a kindergarten and nursery school. In addition, they taught classes in sewing and hygiene, organized discussions and medical lectures for young mothers, opened an art gallery and neighborhood center, offered college extension courses, advocated for neighborhood improvements such as streetlights and paved streets, and supported activities for troubled youths.

Jane Addams, as one of twelve female delegates to the 1912 Republican national convention, seconded the presidential nomination of Theodore Roosevelt, but she would not be able to vote until 1920. In 1931, Jane Addams was awarded the Nobel Peace Prize in Oslo, Norway, receiving worldwide recognition for her life's work. Years before, just after her father's death, she described him as "an uncompromising enemy of wrong and wrongdoing—a fearless advocate of right things in public life."

SOURCES:
Jane Addams—Pioneer for Social Justice, Cornelia Meigs (Little, Brown and Company, Boston, 1970).
Jane Addams, Jane Hovde (Facts on File, New York, 1989).

FAMOUS CHILD:	William "Bill" Bradley
FATHER'S NAME:	Warren Bradley

PAPA SAID: *"I want to sleep at night with a clear conscience and a good name."*

*U*nited States Senator Bill Bradley was taught the value of a dollar and a good reputation early in life. His father was a small-town Missouri banker who had risen through the ranks from an entry-level job "shining pennies" to one as president of the Crystal City State Bank. As bank president, he felt that a special sense of trust had been delegated to him by local depositors and borrowers. Bill states, "His proudest achievement was that throughout the Great Depression he never foreclosed on a single homeowner."

Warren attended his son's basketball games and encouraged him to go to Princeton instead of Duke, where he had been offered a basketball scholarship. Bill suggests his dad was probably disappointed he did not return home to run the bank. He often reminded his all-American and Olympic gold medal–winning offspring that basketball was "just a game" and would ask, "When are you going to get a real job?" Once Bill told his father what he earned as a professional basketball player, however, Warren Bradley, ever the fiscal realist, replied, "Not a bad job."

Elected in 1978 to the United States Senate on the Democratic ticket in New Jersey, Bradley was respected by both sides of the political aisle in Washington. Republican Jack Kemp, in writing a testimonial for Bradley's 1996 book *Time Present, Time Past*, said, "Anyone who loves the country should take a look at it through Bill Bradley's eyes." Behind those eyes are values from his Missouri childhood.

Bill Bradley explains, "My mother always wanted me to be a success. My father always wanted me to be a gentleman. Neither wanted me to be a politician." He adds that nothing was more important to his father than "a good credit rating, keeping your word, saving your money, and never getting close to the 'unethical.'"

SOURCE:
Time Present, Time Past, Bill Bradley (Alfred A. Knopf, New York, 1996).

FAMOUS CHILD:	Clara Barton
	(Clarissa Harlowe Barton)
FATHER'S NAME:	Captain Stephen Barton

PAPA SAID: *"Serve your country with all you have; seek and comfort the afflicted everywhere; honor God and love mankind."*

C aptain Stephen Barton came home from the military to become a moderator of town meetings, selectman, captain of the militia, and later a representative to the Massachusetts General Court. His philanthropy led him to donate funds to the poor and to found a "house for destitute families" in his town of North Oxford, Massachusetts. Clara described her father as "a calm, sound, reasonable, high-toned, moral man."

Clara grew up in a household of eccentric and colorful personalities much older than herself. Her father's war stories and "boys' activities" dominated her childhood, leading

Stephen Barton to describe his daughter as "more boy than girl." The bright, hardworking, and sensitive child increasingly spent time out in the community helping relatives and families in need.

Clara got a job teaching, but soon became fascinated with the military and the assistance she could give to those at "the front." To a cousin she wrote, "Why can't I come and have a tent there and take care of your poor sick fellows?"

During her father's final illness in 1862, Clara Barton listened to his last instruction to "serve your country with all you have; seek and comfort the afflicted everywhere; honor God and love mankind." As he finished his words, according to author Elizabeth Brown Prior, he handed Clara his gold Masonic badge to wear for luck and protection.

After his death and inspired by his advice, she pleaded tearfully with Colonel Daniel Rucker to be allowed to go to the front with hospital supplies for Civil War casualties. He agreed, allowing Clara Barton to pass through the lines "with such stores as she may wish to take for the comfort of the sick and wounded."

Later known as the Angel of the Battlefield, Clara went on to found the American Red Cross before she died in 1912. Author Prior concludes, "A strong current of philanthropy ran in her family's blood; she honored charity because her father had encouraged her to do so, and she lived what he had taught."

SOURCE:
Clara Barton, Professional Angel, Elizabeth Brown Prior (University of Pennsylvania Press, Philadelphia, 1987).

FAMOUS CHILD:	Benjamin Franklin
FATHER'S NAME:	Josiah Franklin

PAPA... *"always took care to start some useful topic for Discourse which might tend to improve the Minds of his Children."*
(Ben Franklin)

osiah Franklin emigrated from the English Midlands to the colonies in 1683 and spent most of his life a candle maker and skilled mechanic, supporting a family that eventually included thirteen children. Benjamin, the seventh child of Josiah's second marriage, stated that his father's "great Excellence lay in sound understanding and solid judgment." He went on to say that his father was "ingenious, could draw prettily, and was skill'd in Music." Many people consulted him and asked for his opinion "in Affaires of the Town or Church," and he was "frequently chosen as Arbitrator."

Benjamin Franklin, with less than two years of formal schooling, devoured books of all kinds and apprenticed to his father in the candle-making business: cutting wicks, filling molds, tending shop, and running errands. Later, when he secretly left Boston for Philadelphia, his father was upset, preferring instead that he study for the ministry. In Philadelphia, Benjamin started his newspaper, the *Pennsylvania Gazette*, and printed *Poor Richard's Almanac* in 1732, after having studied for a time in London and having received training as a master printer.

By the end of Benjamin Franklin's career, he had made major contributions to the fields of business, politics, science, philosophy, diplomacy, and invention. Using his father's significant contribution to his own community in colonial Boston as a prototype, Benjamin in turn went on to influence the world.

SOURCE:
Benjamin Franklin—A Biography, Ronald W. Clark (Random House, New York, 1983).

FAMOUS CHILD: George Burns (Nathan Birnbaum)
FATHER'S NAME: Louis P. Birnbaum
PAPA...   *believed "life on earth was just a stopover on our way to the hereafter."*

L ouis Birnbaum married at sixteen in a prearranged marriage in Eastern Europe and two years later emigrated to New York City's Lower East Side. He initially worked twelve-hour days as a pants presser in a city sweatshop to support his wife Dorothy and their twelve children, the ninth of whom would later become known as George Burns. Despite their poor economic status, George recalled, "Whatever they did must have been right, because everyone turned out fine. None of us wound up in jail, none of us were alcoholics, and none of us got mixed up with drugs." George quipped in his autobiography that the reason might have been, "We couldn't afford it."

George noted that his father was a dreamer who spent most of his time at the synagogue reading religious books or discussing philosophy. Louis was a part-time cantor and also earned money hiring himself out as as a "mashgiach" to certify that everything was kosher at various family events in their orthodox synagogue. He would often work for nothing. Once after a High Holiday event, when his wife asked him why he was so happy when he was not paid, Louis replied, "They asked me to come back next year." George's father died at age forty-seven when George was only seven. George recalled with pride the way the community turned out for the funeral, reflecting the respect in which his father was held.

Around the same time, George started a singing career with three friends in a group called the Peewee Quartet. He continued to perform until just before his death at one hundred—singing, acting, joking, commenting, and even playing God in two movies. He noted, "It is true my father may not have provided me with too many material things, but he did give me a sense of responsibility, and he taught me the difference between right and wrong."

SOURCE:
The Third Time Around, George Burns (G. P. Putnam's Sons, New York, 1980).

FAMOUS CHILD: Bernard Baruch

FATHER'S NAME: Simon Baruch

PAPA SAID: *"Do your duty in all things. You could not do more. You might not wish to do less."*

Simon Baruch often quoted these words of General Robert E. Lee to his son, Bernard, and clearly followed them himself in a life defined by commitment and responsibility. After arriving in the United States from Germany in 1855 at fifteen, Simon taught himself English, became a doctor, and administered to southern soldiers during the Civil War. When he was offered a generous salary to relocate from Camden, South Carolina, north to New York City, Simon moved his young family to Washington Heights, where Bernard went to P.S. 69 and later the City College of New York. Soon Bernard got a job as a runner and office boy on Wall Street.

RESPONSIBILITY

At the age of thirty-three, Bernard Baruch was a member of the New York Stock Exchange and on his way to extraordinary financial success. In his long career, Bernard worked with and advised seven Presidents, from Woodrow Wilson to John Kennedy, and was a United States delegate to the Paris Peace Conference. He always, however, had "the example of my father constantly before me, to disturb my mind with the question, 'Now that you have money, what are you going to do with it?'"

Bernard, inspired by his father's sense of duty, always maintained that "public service was so much more satisfying than making money." In the book he dedicated to his parents, *Baruch— My Own Story*, he acknowledged that his father's pioneering in physical medicine and rehabilitation led him many years later to establish the Institute of Physical Medicine and Rehabilitation at Bellevue Hospital.

SOURCE:
Baruch—My Own Story, Bernard M. Baruch (Henry Holt, New York, 1957).

FAMOUS CHILD:	Gordie Howe
FATHER'S NAME:	Albert Howe

PAPA SAID: *"Do you want to play hockey?"*

"Yes," replied sixteen-year-old Gordie.

"Well, I think here's your opportunity. If you don't want to, say so. But I gotta hang that door."

*F*or Minnesota native Albert Howe, life in the Canadian prairie town of Saskatoon, Saskatchewan, was tough, but at least there was land there and a job or two. Through the years, he worked and struggled during tough times as a laborer, horseman, hunter, auto mechanic, and construction worker—proud that he never had to go on welfare to support his nine children. On the day that Gordie Howe was born in 1928, he was on a construction job with his team of horses. Staying home meant not getting paid.

As a child, Gordie Howe was small, frail, thin, and sickly. Oatmeal was a common staple as his parents tried to feed their big family on a tight budget. Lack of variety in his diet led to a calcium deficiency, which was remedied by vitamins and exercise. When Gordie got his first skates at the age of five and a half, he didn't look back and almost "never took the skates off."

One day he went to the store to get some ice cream, but shyly returned home without it, asking his father to get it for him—afraid to ask himself. "You'll wait a long time, boy. You got to go in there and hustle for yourself." For the sixth of nine children, it was a tough lesson to learn, but for his independent, tough, and responsible father, it was the only one.

Gordie eventually grew up as independent as his dad—swimming, fishing, riding logs in the river, and pursuing the sport of hockey on his own. Although he gained strength and confidence as he grew older, a process helped immeasurably by his involvement in a competitive and rigorous sport, Gordie always remained soft-spoken and kind, according to author Roy Macskimming. The resourceful boy taped and retaped broken hockey sticks and used magazines and catalogues as shin pads. Lack of equipment, he'd determined, would never interfere with his future success.

As Gordie matured and grew stronger, he worked on his father's construction crew lifting ninety-pound cement bags. His son was now as strong as he was and responsible enough to hold a real job, and Albert Howe was proud. But before long, at the age of sixteen, Gordie had a decision to make. Should he go to the 1944 Red Wings training camp in Windsor, Ontario? Dad didn't have an opinion one way or another. It was Gordie's decision and Albert had work to do.

Before his seventeenth birthday, Gordie Howe signed with the Detroit Red Wings. Over a long career, he was the leading scorer six times on his way to accruing 801 National Hockey League goals. No longer a small, frail child, Gordie Howe at fifty-one played for the Hartford Whalers alongside his own sons, Mark and Marty.

SOURCE:
Gordie—A Hockey Legend, Roy Macskimming (Greystone Books, Toronto, 1994).

FAMOUS CHILD: Charlton Heston

FATHER'S NAME: Chet Heston

PAPA SAID: *"I'm not taking any relief handout, ever! You hear me?"*

For the first ten years of his life, Charlton Heston lived an idyllic life with his family in a northern Chicago suburb on a shore of Lake Michigan. Charlton, referring to his childhood memories as "thick with trees," enjoyed hunting, fishing, and chopping wood. This was before the word "divorce" entered his young life.

Suddenly, his father was gone. Charlton moved to Columbus, Georgia, to live with his aunt and cousins until his parents' divorce was final, returning to St. Helen, Michigan, during the winter. Before long a family friend, Chet Heston, became his stepfather, and the young family moved to Alliance, Ohio, where

Chet had hopes of finding work during the depths of the Depression.

In no time, Chet had found work to support his new family, rented a room in an old house, and given young Charlton his last name, while conscientiously paying the rent on time and always seeing that food was on the table.

Once during the same summer, Charlton went down to the town's relief office with two stepcousins to pick up free food. When Chet heard about it, he made it very clear exactly why this was not acceptable. The hardworking and proud head of the Heston family was not going to let his stepchildren go on welfare. Charlton Heston says, "I admire Chet Heston more for his desperate odyssey that summer than for anything else I know about him; he never quit."

By the time that difficult summer was over, Chet had found a more permanent position in Wilmette, Illinois, and eventually obtained an executive position in a defense plant during the war, while Charlton was discovering as a teenager the sophisticated drama program at New Trier High School. "They gave me the center of my life: my work," Charlton explains.

When Chet Heston had a heart attack twenty years later, Charlton said he was "proud to pay off the last of the mortgage and give my mother the deed to the house he'd worked so hard to provide." Charlton Heston expended as much effort in his film career as his stepfather had expended in keeping the rent paid and food on the table. Chet's reward? Charlton carries his name proudly.

SOURCE:
In the Arena, Charlton Heston (Simon & Schuster, New York, 1995).

Famous Child:	Walter Elias Disney
Father's Name:	Elias Disney

Papa Said: *"Walter, the head of the O'Zell has a job for you down there. It will pay you twenty-five dollars a week."*

*I*f eighteen-year-old Walter had taken that job at the O'Zell jelly factory upon his return from the World War I Red Cross Ambulance Corps, Mickey Mouse might have been a character on a jelly jar. At the time his son's refusal seemed stupid to the ever-practical Elias, who felt that a real job was something to value. Walter, however, who had decorated his ambulances with cartoon characters, informed his father that he wanted to be an artist instead.

This wasn't the first conflict between Walt and his dad. The perfectionist, short-tempered Elias Disney saw these characteristics in his son and wasn't always happy about it. When one of his children would do wrong, he'd exclaim, "Great Scott!" or "Land o' Goshen!" His five children soon learned that his way was the only way to do something. Despite their conflicts, however, Walt Disney would later admit, "I had tremendous respect for my dad. Nothing but his family counted."

Elias held several jobs to support his family, which required that they move from place to place. He once ran a two-thousand-subscriber newspaper route while hiring Walt as one of his unpaid delivery boys. Elias never believed in paying his sons for chores, assuming that the money would be spent on frivolities. The enterprising young Walter, in a hint of his future acumen for business, often sold an additional fifty papers behind his father's back, pocketing the extra earnings for himself.

During their years on a Missouri farm, young Walt developed his interest in drawing farm animals, and later, with his father's consent, he took Saturday classes at the Kansas City Art Institute. By 1923, once his talents had developed through a few jobs in commercial art, he and his brother Roy decided to start the Disney Brothers Studio. After obtaining a $2,500 loan from their parents, Walt told his dad, "I'll make the Disney name famous around the world."

SOURCE:
The Man Behind the Magic—The Story of Walt Disney, Katherine and Richard Greene (Viking Penguin, New York, 1991).

FAMOUS CHILD: Wilbur and Orville Wright

FATHER'S NAME: Milton Wright

PAPA SAID: *"I want you to show the foreigners that you are teetotalers, and in every way maintain that high character that is most proper to have, and which in the eyes of the best in America is the most approved."*

ilton Wright was proud. In 1903, his sons, Orville and Wilbur, had been the first people to ever fly a self-propelled aircraft, at Kitty Hawk, North Carolina. They were now in Europe to promote the machine in a highly publicized tour. To this clergyman who'd moonlighted as a teacher and farmer to support his family in the early years, reputation had everything to do with success.

Orville and Wilbur grew up puttering around with mechanical devices—to the delight of their dad. They made woodcuts with engraving tools, adapted and built their own printing press, developed their own glass plates to develop photos in their darkroom, and turned wood on a lathe. The boys were always experimenting. As teens, they started their own publishing company and put out a newspaper, and when the bicycle was just becoming popular, the boys began selling, then manufacturing them at the Wright Cycle Company.

Then, in 1896, they heard about European experiments with sustained flight. Nothing else mattered now. They were obsessed, and started experimenting with kites and gliders. A short seven years later in Kitty Hawk, their plane actually flew.

Shortly before Wilbur died at forty-four, he recalled, "Orville and myself lived together, played together, worked together, and in fact thought together." When his will was read, Wilbur had a special final message for his father: "My earnest thanks for his example of a courageous, upright life."

Orville went on to live until 1948, when throughout Dayton, Ohio, citizens stopped to remember the aviation pioneers who'd worked so long and hard trying to fly their kites and gliders in the cow pasture outside of town.

SOURCE:
Wilbur and Orville Wright, Fred Howard (Alfred A. Knopf, New York, 1987).

FAMOUS CHILD:	John Mohler Studebaker
FATHER'S NAME:	John Studebaker
PAPA SAID:	*"Owe no man anything but to love one another."*

hese words were inscribed over the door of John Studebaker's brand-new blacksmith shop for all to see. By 1835, he had just finished building the shop near the town of Ashland, Ohio, but didn't realize just how soon his philosophy would have to be tested.

Before the panic of 1837, the young blacksmith and wagon builder from a German Pennsylvania family had extended credit to family and friends, who were subsequently unable to pay their bills. John, however, had bills to pay himself. Author Edwin Corle explains, "John Studebaker's name on an obligation meant that John Studebaker would meet that obligation." So he sold his property and mortgaged his land to pay the debts. The result? Years of hard work.

Seeking opportunity, he left his sons in charge of the business and went farther west. The town of South Bend, Indiana, looked promising, and in 1851, the family arrived there in a covered wagon they had built themselves. In 1852, John's sons, Henry and Clem Studebaker, rented a shop and started a firm called H. & C. Studebaker. They later involved John M. Studebaker and two of their other brothers in the business as well.

With his father's advice to guide him, John M. Studebaker shared with his brothers a vision of the rapid expansion of transportation, in part fueled by the gold rush. By 1860, the business was a going concern, with fourteen workmen, a manufacturing shop, a lumberyard, and a sales force. With continued hard work, the brothers lived to see the first Studebaker-built automobile, sporting two cylinders and sixteen horses, sold at the factory gate in 1904 for $2,000. Over the next six years, 2,481 Studebakers were sold.

After the last brother's death in 1917, the company, still family-run, continued to produce cars, but it merged with Packard in 1954, and the last Studebaker—with its classic front-end design—came off the line in 1963.

SOURCE:
John Studebaker—An American Dream, Edwin Corle (E. P. Dutton, New York, 1948).

FAMOUS CHILD: "Yogi" Berra (Lawrence Peter Berra)

FATHER'S NAME: Pietro Berra

PAPA SAID: *"Playing baseball or playing anything else wasn't good. Work was good."*

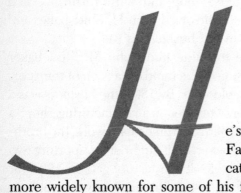

He's in the baseball Hall of Fame, but former Yankee catcher Yogi Berra is probably more widely known for some of his famous sayings, such as "It ain't over till it's over," or "Baseball is ninety percent mental; the other half is physical."

While Yogi didn't get his love of baseball or his folksy perspective from his immigrant father, he combined his desire to please his father with his father's Depression-based work ethic in creating the foundation for his entire career.

Yogi said, "Wanting to make my folks happy and proud was important to me, and was important until the day they died."

RESPONSIBILITY

Even as a sixty-three-year-old, Yogi carried a photo of his parents in his wallet. He knew the pride both of them felt when they first saw his name in the newspaper and remembered his dad's happiness as he'd gather with friends in his St. Louis home to watch Yogi and the Yankees on television.

Lawrence Berra developed a love for baseball while growing up in the Italian immigrant section of St. Louis known as Dago Hill, where baseball catcher and broadcaster Joe Garagiola was a neighborhood friend and teammate. After a childhood teammate noticed that Lawrence sat on the bench the same way a Hindu spiritual leader sat in a recent movie he had seen, Lawrence forever had the nickname "Yogi."

Yogi Berra dropped out of school in the eighth grade to support his family during the Great Depression. He sold newspapers and even boxed for a while, winning eight out of nine bouts. His baseball skills, however, eventually attracted the most attention. He soon had a Yankee contract offer of $90 a month and a $500 bonus. His professional baseball career had begun.

Yogi applied his dad's work ethic to baseball, and by the time he retired to a baseball managerial job twenty years later, he had been named to fifteen All-Star teams and had played in a record fourteen World Series.

In classic Yogi language, he dedicated his book, *Yogi: It Ain't Over . . .* , to his parents with the words, "To my mother, who felt the two most beautiful buildings in the world were St. Peter's in Rome and Yankee Stadium in the Bronx. To my dad, who took her to St. Peter's once and to Yankee Stadium fifty-seven times." It appears that Yogi's success finally convinced his dad that work applied to baseball was indeed good.

SOURCES:

Yogi: It Ain't Over . . . , Yogi Berra with Tom Horton (McGraw-Hill, New York, 1989).

Baseball Legends—Yogi Berra, Marty Appel (Chelsea House Publishers, New York, 1992).

FAMOUS CHILD:	Trisha Yearwood (Patricia Yearwood)
FATHER'S NAME:	Jack Yearwood

PAPA SAID: *"No daughter of mine would drop out of school to chase some far-fetched dream."*

J ack Yearwood, son of a hardworking Georgia family, was always supportive of his daughter's interest in music. He frequently called his two daughters out to perform for dinner guests and watched with pride as they sang in church groups and for town meetings in tiny Monticello, Georgia. Jack Yearwood, however, was not a stage father who sacrificed other family values for a dream.

For Trisha, music was just that—a dream, which started with an Elvis Presley album that she was given by a friend at age five and her family's collection of country music records highlighting

Patsy Cline and Hank Williams. By thirteen, she had taught herself to play the guitar and sang Linda Ronstadt duets with her sister.

She completed junior college and then transferred to the University of Georgia, but Trisha informed her parents after her first semester that she would not return. Author Lisa Gubernick observes that while her disappointed parents did not want to "derail their daughter's dreams, they just wanted to discipline them." It was therefore agreed that Trisha would transfer to a music business program at Belmont College in Nashville in 1985. Sending Trisha to Nashville had the same effect as Miles Davis' father's sending young Miles to the jazz center of New York, for as she pursued her studies at Belmont College, she also absorbed the country music all around her in Nashville.

By 1992, Yearwood had a contract with MCA and had recorded an album that sold millions, had won the Academy of Country Music Award for new artists, and had received two Grammy nominations. Her parents now operate the Trisha Yearwood Fan Club from their home in Monticello.

Yearwood notes her parents' role in both her career and her solid professional reputation. "I was the girl from the small-town Georgia family. You don't rock the boat. No one talked about me because there was nothing to say. I had respect for my parents and still do. I still feel a responsibility to them. I don't want to do something that would make them be disappointed in me."

SOURCE:
Trisha Yearwood, The Making of a Nashville Star, Lisa Rebecca Gubernick (William Morrow, New York, 1993).

SELF-DISCIPLINE

Oprah Winfrey
Marvin Hamlisch
Katharine Hepburn
Pope John Paul II
Wilma Rudolph
Nancy Kerrigan
Fiorello La Guardia
Bob Dylan
Oliver Stone
Carl Sandburg
Steven Spielberg
Mickey Mantle
Liberace

 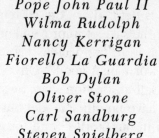
 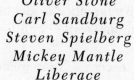

SELF-DISCIPLINE

*S*elf-discipline is defined as "the correction of government of oneself for the sake of improvement." Benjamin Franklin told us how "each year, one vicious habit rooted out in time ought to make the worst man good." Oliver Goldsmith warned us of the dangers of self-absorption when he said, "People seldom improve when they have no other model but themselves to copy after." The children in our stories were fortunate: Their models were their fathers.

One way a father teaches self-discipline is to teach his child the rules. Vernon Winfrey had a problem. He hadn't seen his daughter in years, but here she was on his doorstep at the age of fourteen. His mission was a tough one, for she was a stranger to rules. With a dose of firmness sprinkled with love, however, Vernon set them down—lots of them. His daughter, Oprah Winfrey, grew up and later thanked him for his effort.

Achille La Guardia was exasperated as he dropped his son off on his first day of school. There was just no controlling this boy. The Italian immigrant was mortified—he valued conforming to his new country's culture. Fiorella La Guardia grew up not only to follow a few rules, but to develop out of his early stubbornness an impressive ability to lead. As mayor of New York City in the thirties, he led reforms that modernized the city and did much to alleviate its overwhelming social problems.

A father often guides or nudges his child to learn while speaking the same words Mickey Mantle's father used: "Practice, practice, practice." Few young children can look far enough down the road to see the rewards of hard work. Max Hamlisch explained to his young son that musical training had to start early to get into the blood. Years later, his son Marvin, by then at the top of his discipline as a musician, understood exactly what he meant. Mutt Mantle lived baseball, enough to have almost been a professional player himself. Admonishing his son to practice, Mutt watched his son achieve in a discipline he dearly loved, and just before his death, Mutt watched that son, Mickey, hit a home run in the 1952 World Series.

Sometimes a child simply watches a self-disciplined father and learns that way. He doesn't need quite as much nudging and accomplishes an extraordinary feat, such as winning an Olympic medal. Dan Kerrigan worked hard—he had to earn money to pay for his daughter's ice-skating lessons. Working as a welder and moonlighting by driving an ice-resurfacing machine at the skating rink, he got by. Nancy Kerrigan, as one of the top figure skaters in the world, accomplished it all with an extraordinary display of self-discipline that was not so very different from her father's. Ed Rudolph struggled to support his twenty-two children, and he wouldn't accept welfare to help him. His daughter had polio and wore a leg brace until she was ten. By the seventh grade she'd gotten tired of being and feeling disabled. With extraordinary determination, she forced herself to walk without the brace, and in the 1956 Olympics won a bronze medal in track. Ed lived just long enough to see his daughter, Wilma Rudolph, win three gold medals in the 1960 Olympics.

The fathers in our stories inspired their children to muster enough discipline to control their behaviors, develop their talents, or overcome a life challenge. In learning this self-mastery, their children were in a perfect position to accomplish and enjoy future success.

FAMOUS CHILD: Oprah Gail Winfrey

FATHER'S NAME: Vernon Winfrey

PAPA SAID: *"Be home by midnight or, by God, sleep on the porch!"*

I t took a while for Oprah to find her place in the world. Born in Kosciusko, Mississippi, Oprah Winfrey spent her first six years with her grandmother, Hattie Mae. (Oprah's mother, Vernita Lee, left town after the local cotton mill closed down and local jobs dried up, and relocated to Milwaukee.) At the age of six, Oprah went to live with her mother, who by now was more financially secure and had a steady boyfriend who promised Vernita Lee that he would not only marry her, but give the young family a home. The reality, however, was somewhat different.

By the time Oprah turned fourteen, she was not only bright and independent but also headstrong and headed for trouble.

With a mother who worked long days, Oprah had become more and more difficult to parent. She stayed out late or didn't come home at all, hung around with a fast crowd, and eventually ran away for a week. By then, Vernita was desperate, and considered committing Oprah to a home for troubled teens. She pleaded with the girl's birth father, Vernon Winfrey, and his wife, Zelma, to take her. They did. Author George Mair opines, "It was the best decision of Oprah's teenage years."

Vernon Winfrey, a barbershop owner, very quickly set down strict rules for fourteen-year-old Oprah to follow, coupled with a strong dose of loving guidance. In the first "real home" she had ever known, Oprah learned all about curfews, discipline, hard work, dress codes, and good grades. At Vernon and Zelma's insistence, Oprah learned twenty new words a week and wrote five book reports every two weeks—all enforced not by physical punishments, but by stern lectures.

The results were remarkable. With her newly acquired self-discipline, the bright young teenager proceeded to become student council president, was chosen to attend a White House Conference on Youth in Colorado, represented East Nashville High in a national speaking contest, and in her senior year was elected Most Popular Girl by her classmates. Firmly guided into a habit of reading by her father and stepmother, Oprah was inspired by the writings of Sojourner Truth, Harriet Tubman, Alice Walker, and Maya Angelou. She excelled in school speaking classes and theater arts, and landed a job in radio broadcasting at the age of seventeen.

Vernon and Zelma Winfrey, faced with a young daughter headed for trouble, had committed themselves in a major way to her development and subsequent self-discipline. With a background as a dishwasher, janitor, church deacon, and city councilman in Nashville, Vernon Winfrey may have taken on the most difficult—and certainly the most important—job of his life: the father of a teen in trouble. On a wall of his barbershop, which still existed in Nashville in 1992, are the words: "Attention, Teenagers: If You Are Tired of Being Hassled by Unreasonable Parents, Now Is the Time for Action! Leave Home and Pay Your Own Way While You Still Know Everything."

In 1987, Oprah gave the commencement address at Tennessee State University and received her undergraduate degree, after having dropped out to pursue a career in radio many years before. That day she endowed ten scholarships worth $770,000 in her father's name and could finally say to this man who'd been so dedicated to his daughter's education, "See, Daddy, I amounted to something." Today Oprah says, "My father turned my life around by insisting I be more than I was and by believing I could be more."

SOURCE:
Oprah Winfrey—The Real Story, George Mair (Birch Lane Press, 1994).

FAMOUS CHILD:	Marvin Hamlisch
FATHER'S NAME:	Max Hamlisch

PAPA SAID: *"Marvin, you are probably too young to understand this. What I'm giving you is a rare thing. I never had the chance myself. Musical training has to start young. It has to get into your blood. Over and over and over, practice, practice, practice. Marvin, I know you like to write songs, and the better pianist you are, the better you can play them. Years from now, you'll know what all this means."*

I n the mid-1930s, as a Jew in prewar Austria, Max Hamlisch left behind a successful music career and took to America his love of the old-world culture and the music of Schubert, Schumann, and Strauss.

After his son Marvin was born in 1944, it took Max only six years to set him on the way to a career in music by enrolling the boy in piano lessons at The Juilliard School of Music in New York. While young Marvin went to public school, he spent his Saturdays attending classes in music theory, sight reading, and harmony.

In his memoir, Hamlisch modestly notes that he realized at the age of seven that he was never going to be a great concert-pianist, and that while Juilliard's primary goal seemed to be to create great instrumentalists, he was more interested in writing songs. He adds, "If I practiced one hour daily, that was a lot. But after that hour there was plenty of time to play songs I heard or songs I wrote." The sound-isolated Juilliard practice rooms enabled him to do this unbeknownst to his teachers, fellow students, or father. Although struggling with his father's message of self-discipline Marvin Hamlisch continued creating melodies, a talent that would eventually become the basis of his long career in music.

Hamlisch recalls, "From the time I could play the piano, I remember trying to write tunes." He adds that while his father realized he would never be another Horowitz, he still prodded him to "practice, practice, practice," creating little games and incentives to encourage him. Probably as a result, Marvin practiced with enough self-discipline to pass the required exams while maintaining his Juilliard scholarship for fourteen years.

Max Hamlisch's advice to his son was given when he and ten-year-old Marvin, while waiting for the boy's scholarship audition, found themselves locked out of a Juilliard building and on the building's roof. While they waited, Marvin had asked Max why he had to go through this, and his father noted the importance of maximizing his God-given skills. The future composer of Broadway shows and more than forty motion picture scores—including the Oscar-winning score for *The Way We Were* and the adaptation of Scott Joplin's music for *The Sting*—said years later that that time on the roof with his father was probably the most important fifty minutes of his career.

SOURCE:
The Way I Was, Marvin Hamlisch with Gerald Gardner (Charles Scribner's Sons, New York, 1992).

FAMOUS CHILD:	Katharine Houghton Hepburn
FATHER'S NAME:	Dr. Norval Thomas "Tom" Hepburn

PAPA SAID: *"All right, I'll give you fifty dollars to help pay your expenses for a couple weeks, until you recover from this madness, but that's the last penny you'll get from me until you do something respectable."*

D r. Tom Hepburn called his young daughter Redtop and spent hours constructing a stage for their backyard so that she could put on plays. He created "chores" so she could earn money to buy fan magazines or go to the movies. He delighted in her individualism, independence, and intelligence. She struggled in her sophomore year at Bryn Mawr College, with inconsistent grades, few close friends, and no long-term goal, according to author Anne Edwards. By the fall of her junior year, however, she'd changed her major from history to English and decided to pursue an acting career; and, with a self-discipline learned at her father's knee, she directed all of her energy toward this goal. Soon, her grades improved and she had the lead in two plays, plus friends with the same interests as she. The self-assured and independent Kate Hepburn had found her calling.

After graduation, Katharine accepted a job in a stock company in Baltimore. Dr. Hepburn, according to biographer Anne Edwards, was both "stunned and furious," prompting his remark, "You want to be an actress only because it is the easiest and most conspicuous way to show off!" It was then that Dr. Hepburn begrudgingly offered to help pay her expenses for a couple of weeks—until she found "something respectable."

It was hard for Dr. Hepburn to understand such artistic pursuits. He had graduated from Johns Hopkins in Baltimore, done an internship at Hartford Hospital in Connecticut, and spent a long and successful career in Hartford as a surgeon. He was the traditional "head of the house." He was self-disciplined and his intellectual standards were high. He was the son of an Episcopal clergyman. And now his daughter wanted to make a career out of what he considered a frivolous hobby.

Nonetheless, throughout Kate Hepburn's life and career, she maintained close contact with her father, who may have had strong opinions, but remained interested in her achievements. When he ultimately saw how happy she was and how successful she had become, Dr. Hepburn was very proud.

In an interview in 1975 with writer Ralph Martin, referring

to her frequent visits to her parents' home in West Hartford, Connecticut, Kate Hepburn said, "I kept my life there, my roots. . . . And when I went back there I didn't go to *my* atmosphere: I went to *their* atmosphere—of which I was a part. I was going to my father's house. . . . That's very unusual, isn't it? Very, very unusual that someone who's sort of made it in the big world could still want to go home to their father's house?"

SOURCE:
A Remarkable Woman, Anne Edwards (William Morrow, New York, 1985).

FAMOUS CHILD:	Karol "Lolek" Jozef Wojtyla (Pope John Paul II)
FATHER'S NAME:	Karol Wojtyla

PAPA... *"was a loving father but a stern disciplinarian."*
(Pope John Paul II)

The man who was to be Pope was born in Wadowice, Poland, on May 18, 1920. While the family was not well-off financially, matters were worsened when nine-year-old Karol's mother Emilia died in childbirth and an older brother died a few years later.

Lolek (diminutive for Karol) was a very bright student who excelled at whatever he tried. However, his father, a former Polish Army officer, kept close rein on the young man, mapping out each day in a very controlled schedule that included Mass, school, a meal, an hour of free time, and homework.

Young Lolek and his father were very close and moved to Cracow when Lolek enrolled at the renowned University Jagiellonian. He excelled in drama and was considering an acting career when Hitler invaded Poland in 1939. Subsequently, Karol Senior was killed and the future Pope was forced to work in a stone quarry. His father's death left him without a family in the dismal period of the Nazi occupation.

While working in the resistance movement, Karol Wojtyla found inspiration in the story of St. John of the Cross, a sixteenth-century Spanish mystic and poet who had written of the *via negativa*—a darkness in which God is found after the soul has been rid of all delight in the senses. He turned to the church in 1942 and, at great risk, enrolled in a seminary, which was illegal under the Nazi rules for native Poles.

With a self-discipline learned at an early age from his father, Lolek Wojtyla began his studies. Ordained into the priesthood in 1946, he became archbishop of Cracow in 1964, a cardinal in 1967, and in 1978 was named the first Polish Pope. His papacy has been marked by two primary directions, a vigorous commitment to world peace, and the full implementation of the controlling doctrines of the 1965 Second Vatican Council, which set down many disciplinary rules and resisted innovations.

SOURCE:
Man from a Far Country: An Informal Portrait of Pope John Paul II, Mary Craig (William Morrow, New York, 1979).

FAMOUS CHILD:	Wilma Rudolph
FATHER'S NAME:	Ed Rudolph

PAPA SAID: *"If you get a whipping at school, the first thing you can expect when you get home is another one."*

*S*ixteen-year-old Wilma, having survived the Olympic trials in Seattle, was the youngest member of the 1956 Olympics, and a bronze medal was her reward. In the 1960 Olympics, Wilma ran fast enough to win three Olympic gold medals. The story gets even more interesting when one learns about all the life challenges that she'd met in order to reach the Olympics in the first place.

Born the twentieth of twenty-two children in a loving but poor home in Clarksville, Tennessee, Wilma remembers a houseful of relatives and friends, happy times at Christmas, and at the Clarksville County Fair. Ed Rudolph, a railroad porter and handyman, was with the support of his wife the undisputed head of the household, and was too proud to accept welfare during hard times. He "laid down the rules," was proud of his children, insisted that they respect adults, and was always proud that not one of them had a police record. On Sundays the family went to church while Ed admonished any stragglers with: "No church on Sunday mornings, no nothing else."

From birth, Wilma had a crooked leg that she had always been told was a result of polio. The thin, sickly young child wore a heavy metal brace until she was almost ten, necessitating that she start school later than most children and that, once there, she struggle for acceptance. By the seventh grade, Wilma had gotten "mad about it all" and decided that she would "beat her illnesses no matter what." With a determination and self-discipline that would follow her to the Olympics, she "forced" herself to walk normally without her brace and then discovered basketball. Later, Wilma won every high school running race she entered and discovered that winning felt terrific.

Before the 1960 Olympics, Wilma's dad, by then failing in health, wished her well while telling her not to worry about him— "Just go and run. I'll be here when you get back." Within months, he died, but not until after he'd witnessed her Olympic success.

SOURCE:
Wilma—The Story of Wilma Rudolph, Wilma Rudolph (Times Mirror, New York, 1977).

FAMOUS CHILD: Nancy Kerrigan

FATHER'S NAME: Dan Kerrigan

PAPA SAID: *"If she can just hold it together until tomorrow, we'll be all set."*

*F*ans in Prague and around the world witnessed, in person or on television, one of the top ice-skating competitions—the 1993 World Championships. Dan Kerrigan also watched as his daughter, Nancy, competed against Ukraine's Oksana Baiul and France's Surya Bonaly, and it didn't look good. At twenty-three, Nancy faced a most difficult competition, and although she'd finished first in the technical program, the pressure was mounting.

By the time Dan Kerrigan's "tomorrow" arrived, his daughter had stumbled during her performance, falling to fifth overall and dashing her hopes for top billing. Then later the very same year, at the national championship in Detroit, Dan Kerrigan lifted

Nancy off the stadium floor after she had been assaulted by a man swinging a metal rod at her knee, bruising her kneecap and interrupting the intense training regimen that she had hoped would lead to the Lillehammer (Norway) Olympics in 1994. The dream of victory that Dan and his daughter had worked so hard for was about to fade.

With lots of self-discipline, Dan Kerrigan had worked several jobs, taken loans, and always done whatever it took to pay for his daughter's ice-skating instruction. He also did the cooking at home, for his wife was almost totally blind. Now his daughter's future as a world-class skater, and his dreams for her, were in jeopardy.

After the Detroit nationals were over, the United States Figure Skating Association selected Nancy to represent the United States at the coming Olympics, in spite of her serious injury. The rest was up to her.

With a self-discipline modeled so well by her father, Nancy Kerrigan renewed her commitment to her sport. Within two weeks she had resumed practicing difficult jumps, and in a few more weeks the stiffness in her knee had disappeared, leaving her ready and eager to compete. As her family watched nearby, Nancy Kerrigan skated a performance worthy of a silver medal at the 1994 Lillehammer Olympics.

SOURCE:
Dreams of Gold, Wayne Coffey and Filip Bondy (St. Martin's Press, New York, 1994).

FAMOUS CHILD: Fiorello H. La Guardia

FATHER'S NAME: Achille La Guardia

PAPA SAID: *"He is a bad boy. You can beat this child whenever necessary, although I doubt it will do any good."*

Achille La Guardia had worked hard to get to his position as U.S. Army bandmaster and musician. As an immigrant from southern Italy, he'd experienced discrimination. His son, therefore, must be a full-fledged American. Achille had determined the boy must speak English and go to church. He must learn the rules. He must fit in.

Fiorello, however, was rambunctious, headstrong, and difficult to discipline. With a strict, traditional fathering style consistent with the times, Achille turned to his son's teacher with this advice. Years later, the teacher remembered the six-year-old's strong words as he pulled away from his father, and as he subsequently sat down quietly in his chair.

The headstrong Fiorello resisted his father's church, his discipline, and eventually school, but loved the freedom of growing up an Army brat in Prescott, Arizona. With extraordinary self-discipline, Fiorello, although never having graduated from high school, put himself through law school. Author Thomas Kessner relates that "as much as he resented Achille's austere discipline, Fiorello grew into a strong, resilient boy, with a generous streak of his father's forceful personality." This is exactly what it took for Mayor Fiorello La Guardia to reform and build a modern New York City.

When he was elected mayor in 1934, New York City had overwhelming social problems. He was not only able to shape the government to meet each crisis head-on, but was also poised to help the city focus toward the future. No institution was spared in the process. He investigated and reformed the corrupt courts, fought ethnic prejudice, declared war on government corruption and gambling, and embraced and assisted hundreds of thousands of people out of work during the Depression—accomplishing all this with a lifelong disdain for "professional politicians." Kessner concludes, "Fiorello La Guardia was essentially a product of the interplay between the free, open environment of the West that he came to love, the overbearing influence of his father, and a family tradition of continental culture."

SOURCE:
Fiorello H. La Guardia and the Making of Modern New York, Thomas Kessner (McGraw-Hill, New York, 1989).

FAMOUS CHILD:	Bob Dylan (Robert A. Zimmerman)
FATHER'S NAME:	Abraham Zimmerman

PAPA SAID: *"Some of those people out there make as much money as I do, Bobby. They just don't know how to manage it."*

B ob Dylan's 1964 hit album, *The Times They Are A-Changin'*, made him a spokesperson for a restless and rebellious generation. In many ways its title symbolized the earlier conflict between Bob and his father, Abe Zimmerman.

For Minnesota small-town retail businessman Abe Zimmerman, customers were expected to pay their bills, and his son was expected to follow in his footsteps in the family business. He introduced his teenage son to the business by sending him out to collect on overdue accounts. Bob, however, had a problem that kept him from being a good businessman—he tended to sympathize with his customers. That's when Abe reminded him of the importance of managing money. The message landed on deaf ears at the time. His independent and talented son felt that what was important was listening to and playing rock and roll music. Like many fathers, Abe saw little good in time spent with a guitar or piano, especially when the music was loud.

A classmate of Bob's recalled, however: "Mr. Zimmerman didn't agree with Bob's goals, but he never stood in Bob's way. He supported Bob in those first years after high school, gave him money and a kind of moral support. He gave Bob his blessings, in a way. I always thought he was just the right kind of father for Bob: strict about a lot of things but never so rigid that Bob would really have to run away."

Bob moved on, first to Minneapolis to college, then in 1961 to Greenwich Village in New York. Bob told his friends of his conflict with his father and his need to leave home. When Bob's music, however, began to receive national acclaim, his father was proud, hanging pictures in his store and displaying albums in the window.

By 1963, a more mature Dylan, now willing to acknowledge his parents, invited them to a Carnegie Hall concert (after which the media were quick to point out his middle-class roots). Dylan's father was proud, but nonetheless remained true to his convictions, asking the performer's wife before the concert if she couldn't get Bob to cut his hair.

Shortly after Abe's death in 1968, Dylan named his newly

born son Seth Abraham, and later on began to study Judaism and Hebrew. Biographer Anthony Scaduto wrote that his newfound spirituality reflected a "search for personal salvation" and brought him "full circle, back to the religion of his father."

SOURCE:
Bob Dylan, An Intimate Biography, Anthony Scaduto (Grosset & Dunlap, New York, 1971).

FAMOUS CHILD: Oliver Stone (William Oliver Stone)
FATHER'S NAME: Louis Stone (Louis Silverstein)
PAPA SAID: *"Every day you should do something that you don't want to do."*

Self-discipline and hard work—that's how Louis Silverstein got where he did. Born of Jewish and French Roman Catholic heritage, Louis entered Yale as a freshman with the new name Louis Stone, taken to avoid discrimination as a Jew. He majored in English literature. When the stock market crashed in 1929, life would never be the same. From that point on, shares Oliver Stone, "Money was his Achilles' heel." The young Yale graduate had a tough time finding a job at first, leading him, according to author James Riordan, to see the world as a "cruel place in which you had to be tough to survive. The philosophy had a profound effect on his son."

As an only child, Oliver Stone was precocious, and at times lonely. His parents entertained a lot, which resulted in even more time alone for the boy. He made up games and kept statistics on sports, and, like his father, played chess and loved anything "military." Each year, he looked forward to visiting his maternal grandparents in France, delighting in the long and drawn-out stories his grandfather would tell. When he saw *On the Waterfront* for the first time, the future movie director was hooked. Stone says, "It's as if the world of imagination was a sanctuary from real life. It was a great escape."

Oliver Stone defends the strict discipline meted out by his father: "My dad was sometimes sarcastic and distant, but he could be very loving at times. He was proud of me. I was the only child and he was afraid I'd get spoiled by my mom, so he would be a little tougher. He was a great writer, in my opinion, very intelligent, and had a great sense of humor."

By the age of fifteen, Oliver Stone's world had fallen apart as his parents divorced. Leaving Yale at the end of his freshman year, Oliver went to Saigon and taught English at a Catholic school for Chinese students before joining the Army. Requesting combat in Vietnam, for which he later was awarded a Bronze Star and Purple Heart, Oliver continued his lifetime habit of writing down his experiences.

With a love for a good story and a self-discipline not unlike his father's, Oliver Stone delves deeply into his past to tell his stories. His screenplay and direction of the 1986 Vietnam War film *Platoon* won four Oscars, including those for best director and best picture. His many movies include *Wall Street*, *JFK*, and *Born on the Fourth of July*, for which he received another Oscar as best director.

SOURCE:
Stone—A Biography of Oliver Stone, James Riordan (Hyperion, New York, 1995).

FAMOUS CHILD:	Carl August Sandburg (Charlie, or "Sharlie")
FATHER'S NAME:	August Sandburg
PAPA SAID:	*"Is there any money in poetry, Sharlie?"*

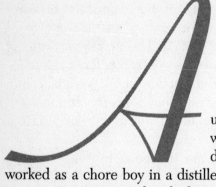

ugust Sandburg didn't get where he got in life by sitting down or by complaining. He worked as a chore boy in a distillery and in a cheese factory and as a construction worker before getting a job as a blacksmith fixing train engines. At the end of the day, he'd march home from the shop covered in grease, only to work on his garden, cut his son's hair, clean the cellar, or perhaps fix something. The closest he ever came to free time was while he was sleeping.

The family's three-room cottage may have needed newspaper pasted to the wall to keep out the winter cold, but at least it was home. It may have been so close to the railroad tracks that the cottage tremored when trains passed, but for one who earned a living fixing train engines, it wasn't a bad place to live. August Sandburg never had time or money for a vacation, but when one lives for one's work, nothing else matters. He never learned to write or speak English very well, but when he called his son's name, "Sharlie" (for Charlie), Carl came, didn't he? There was no need to learn.

The muscular, hardworking man never understood his son's fascination with words. Time spent reading was just one more reason why nothing was getting done and no money was coming in. Young Carl read every chance he got, so his dad's reference to poetry not bringing in enough money to live on made him mad. Carl read about his favorite topics—poetry, history, and geography—while growing up right in the middle of "Lincoln country."

He left school at thirteen and immediately went to work. While at his job in a barbershop at a downtown hotel, Carl listened, watched, and learned. Author W. G. Rogers explains, "Carl Sandburg saw the world with the unspoiled eyes of Carl Sandburg the newsboy, shoeshine boy, window washer, and hired hand." Soon, with the help of railroad passes given to him by his father, the intensely curious Carl started to learn about the physical world outside of Galesburg, Illinois.

With these observations, an intense compassion for the working class, and a work ethic similar to his father's, Carl Sandburg wrote *Chicago Poems* in 1916, then went on to do a biography of Lincoln in two volumes, children's books, and a historical novel, while collecting and singing folk songs, lecturing, studying at college, and telling stories—receiving several Pulitzer Prizes and scores of honors along the way. Rogers points out, "He was as much a laborer at the typewriter as his father [was] at the anvil."

SOURCE:
Carl Sandburg, Yes, W. G. Rogers (Harcourt Brace Jovanovich, New York, 1970).

FAMOUS CHILD:	Steven Spielberg
FATHER'S NAME:	Arnold Spielberg

PAPA SAID: *"I'd help Steven construct sets for his 8mm movies, with toy trucks and papier-mâché mountains. At night I'd tell the kids cliffhanger stories about characters like Joanie Frothy Flakes and Lenny Ludehead."*

*T*he future director of robots, X-wing fighters, and man-made dinosaurs started his film career early in life using an 8mm camera that his mom gave to his dad to record the family's camping adventures. Bored with his father's rather dull movies, young Steven quickly took control of the camera and tried to "get a little more drama into catching a trout."

The camera soon became a toy to replace crayons and charcoal as twelve-year-old Steven documented his own life at twenty-four frames per second. The Oscar-winning director known for films such as *Star Wars*, *Schindler's List*, and *Jurassic Park* stated, "My first real movie was of my Lionel trains crashing into each other. I used to love to stage little wrecks. I'd put my eye right to the tracks and watch the trains crashing."

Biographer Frank Sanello observes that Steven was a "natural cinematographer." Young Spielberg had recognized that by "shooting trains at a low angle, they would appear life-sized on screen."

While his computer engineer dad might have encouraged his camera interest, he was also concerned that this son was having trouble with schoolwork. Steven has said, "From age twelve or thirteen I knew I wanted to be a movie director, and I did not think that science or math or foreign languages were going to help me turn out the little 8mm sagas I was making to avoid homework." He went so far as to take the copy of *The Scarlet Letter* that his father had given him and put stick figures of a bowler knocking down pins on the edge of each page, which then became animated as the pages were turned quickly.

Steven praised his dad's efforts in forcing him to study enough math so he would pass. The man who helped create numerous high-tech movies admits, "I still can't do a fraction," confessing that he continues to occasionally count on his fingers, to his dad's lasting dismay.

Now retired, the elder Spielberg, described by Sanello as "left-brained, analytical, scientific," has twelve patents in his own name and still makes industrial sales films, with the help of advice from his famous son. Sanello gives the father credit for Steven's ability to utilize the "techno wizardry which is the hallmark of most Spielberg films, all those sci-fi epics and scare-'em-to-death roller-coaster rides."

SOURCE:
Spielberg: The Man, the Movies, the Mythology, Frank Sanello (Taylor, Dallas, 1996).

FAMOUS CHILD:	Mickey Mantle
FATHER'S NAME:	Elvin "Mutt" Mantle

PAPA SAID: *"Practice, Practice, Practice. Your belly can wait."*

*I*t might have been time for dinner, but there was always a need for seven-year-old Mickey Mantle to practice hitting a little more. Hit some left-handed against Dad, and then some right-handed against Grandpa, the lefty. That's the way future baseball Hall of Famer Mickey Mantle grew up.

Mickey's dad, "Mutt," was a pretty good baseball player. He played regularly in semipro leagues in rural Oklahoma but never had the opportunity to play on the professional level. From the time he fathered Mickey at eighteen in 1931, his ambition was to make his son a baseball player. In fact, he named him after Hall of Fame catcher Mickey Cochrane.

Mutt had little else in his life. Times were tough during the Depression; he worked in mines or as a tenant farmer, doing what he could to sustain his family. Mickey recalled that despite his father's pressure to make him practice, "Dad always made it seem like fun." By the time he was in second grade he could hit, and by seventeen was attracting attention from professional scouts. The New York Yankees signed him to a minor-league contract right after high school.

Mickey recalled his father's words to his first professional manager, Harry Craft. Mutt said, "I've done all I can for Mickey. I believe he's a good ballplayer and I'm turning him over to you now." He then added to Mickey, "This is your chance, son. Take care of yourself and give 'em hell."

Mutt Mantle was also there to refuel his son's ambition in 1951 when Mickey was going through a slump after being sent back to the minor leagues and was considering quitting baseball. Following a lengthy discussion in which Mutt told him that he thought he "had raised a man, not a coward," Mickey mustered the self-discipline learned at his father's knee and never looked back.

By the fall, Mickey was back in the major leagues with the Yankees. Later, his father, though ill with cancer, came to New York and saw him hit a home run in the 1952 World Series. Mantle observed, "It was the thought of me making good that kept him going." Mutt Mantle died at thirty-nine in 1953. Mickey, of course, went on to hit 536 home runs in a career spanning eighteen years. His 18 World Series home runs, accumulated over a dozen Series, remains a record. He was enshrined in the Baseball Hall of Fame in 1974. In a dedication to his deceased father in his 1985 autobiography, Mantle wrote, "And to my father. I wish he could read this book."

SOURCE:
The Mick, Mickey Mantle with Herb Gluck (Doubleday, Garden City, New York, 1985).

FAMOUS CHILD:	Liberace (Wladziu "Walter" Liberace)
FATHER'S NAME:	Salvatore Liberace

PAPA SAID: *"Children should be learning music by the age of four."*

While flamboyant pianist Liberace's devotion to his mother is legendary, it was his father who introduced him to music and fostered his early development. Salvatore Liberace grew up near Naples, Italy, and studied several instruments, including French horn, at the Formia Municipal School of Music. One of his early jobs was with the John Philip Sousa touring Marine band. Later, when he emigrated to Milwaukee, he insisted the family have a piano.

One day while his older son George was practicing on the violin, Salvatore heard four-year-old Walter repeating George's music on the piano. He was deemed ready for lessons, and soon his sister had to fight for piano practice time. Later, after his thirteen-year-old sister had worked for weeks learning Mendelssohn's *Midsummer Night's Dream* for a recital, Walter picked up the sheet music and learned it in a day. Salvatore Liberace's next move was clear: Despite limited family finances, Salvatore took his talented teenage son to the Wisconsin College of Music and introduced him to Florence Kelly, who remained his teacher for the next seventeen years.

Salvatore was deeply moved when Liberace's playing earned him an opportunity to play with the Chicago Symphony in 1939, for he'd never approved of his son's interest in playing popular music. After the concert the emotional father proclaimed, "Son, I was proud of you. From now on you can play anything you want to. You've proved to me you can do it."

A difficult divorce later separated his parents, resulting in Liberace's longtime devotion to his mother and an estrangement from his father that lasted thirteen years. In 1953, however, a friend secretly arranged to have Salvatore play in the orchestra at one of Liberace's performances in Milwaukee. After both had discovered the setup and the concert had ended, father and son reconciled. They visited each other regularly until Salvatore's death at age ninety-two in 1977.

SOURCE:
Liberace, Bob Thomas (St. Martin's Press, New York, 1987).

INDEX

INDEX

INDEX

INDEX

INDEX

℗ PLUME

LAUGHING AT LIFE

☐ **TURNING 50** *Quotes, Lists, and Helpful Hints* **by William K. Klingaman.** If your birthday candles set off the smoke alarm, don't despair—dig into this warm and funny collection of celebrity quotes, lists, interviews, and tongue-in-cheek advice about the big five-O. Here's all the wit and wisdom of people like Tom Brokaw, Doris Day, Gore Vidal, and Gloria Steinem who have already reached the half-century mark to remind you you're not alone.

(270332—$7.95)

☐ **TURNING 40** *Wit, Wisdom & Whining* **by William K. Klingaman.** Your 40th birthday is the beginning of the rest of your life. And this is the book that delivers the sure-fire, feel-great-about-it attitude you need—good advice, good laughs, and best of all, *lots* of good company. (268214—$8.95)

☐ **ALICE K.'S GUIDE TO LIFE** *One Woman's Tale of Survival—and the Quest for the Perfect Black Shoes* **by Caroline Knapp.** Let Alice K. (not her real initial) show you the way—that is to say, the way she lives and loves or at least does her sometimes bewildered best to. You'll find out the many, *many* aspects of feminine existence far too intimate and delicate—not to mention hilarious—to be specified on the *outside* of a book. (271215—$9.95)

Prices slightly higher in Canada.

Visa and Mastercard holders can order Plume, Meridian, and Dutton books by calling
1-800-253-6476.
They are available at your local bookstore. Allow 4-6 weeks for delivery.
This offer is subject to change without notice.

PL42

DUTTON **PLUME**

QUOTABLES

DUTTON **PLUME**

HEARTWARMING PARENTAL ADVICE

☐ **MOTHER KNEW BEST *Wit and Wisdom from the Moms of Celebrities* by Elsa and David Hornfischer.** 101 marvelous morsels of maternal wisdom! This inspiring collection demonstrates how mothers' words really shaped the lives of the famously successful. Hear from the mothers of Martin Luther King, Jr., Elvis Presley, Muhammad Ali, Mother Teresa, and many more.   (276187—$9.95)

☐ **ZEN AND THE ART OF FATHERHOOD *Lessons from a Master Dad* by Steven Lewis.** This humorous and insightful account mingles hilarious personal recollections from nearly thirty years of parenting with quiet reflections and quotes from admired Zen sages to capture the universal paradoxes, dilemmas, and rewards of fatherhood.   (941479—$19.95)

☐ **FATHERS Compiled and Edited by Jon Winokur.** Bitter or sweet, sentimental and barbed—this compendium of anecdotes, quips, and essays celebrates famous names and ordinary folks. Candice Bergen, Arthur Ashe, Alice Walker, Thurgood Marshall, and more than 200 others remember their fathers to offer moving and humorous testimony to the enduring legacy of fathers.   (272076—$9.95)